# EVERYTHING
# IMUS

# EVERYTHING
# IMUS

*All You Ever Wanted to Know
About Don Imus*

**Jim Reed**

A BIRCH LANE PRESS BOOK
PUBLISHED BY CAROL PUBLISHING GROUP

A Birch Lane Press Book
Published by Carol Publishing Group
Birch Lane Press is a registered trademark of Carol Communications, Inc.

Editorial, sales, and distribution rights and permissions inquiries should be
addressed to Carol Publishing Group, 120 Enterprise Avenue, Secaucus, N.J.
07094

In Canada: Canadian Manda Group, One Atlantic Avenue, Suite 105,
Toronto, Ontario M6K 3E7

Carol Publishing books may be purchased in bulk at special discounts for
sales promotion, fund-raising, or educational purposes. Special editions can
be created to specifications. For details, contact Special Sales Department,
120 Enterprise Avenue, Secaucus, N.J. 07094.

Design by Andrew Gardner
Graphic image on part titles from photo courtesy of author's collection.
Graphic image on sidebars from photo courtesy of © Todd France/Corbis.

Manufactured in the United States of America
10 9 8 7 6 5 4 3 2 1

Library of Congress Cataloging-in-Publication Data

Reed, Jim, 1964–
    Everything Imus : all you ever wanted to know about Don Imus / Jim
Reed.
        p.   cm.
    "A Birch Lane Press book."
    Includes index.
    ISBN 1-55972-504-4 (hardcover)
    1. Imus, Don. 2. Radio broadcasters—United States Biography.
I. Title.
PN1991.4.I48R44   1999
791.44'028'092—dc21
    [B]                                                    99-17691
                                                              CIP

*To Tammy, who makes each day the happiest yet,*
*and*
*To Jack, who may be a bigger fan than I am*

# CONTENTS

# ACKNOWLEDGMENTS

I would have never been able to do this work, especially in just seven months, without the help of many, many people.

Thanks to those listeners who are as crazy about Imus as I am. Every time I would put a strange query into the Internet news groups, people whom I would come to know as just "StatmanJS" or "MissVicki" and their other associates would know the answer that would help me dig a little deeper into Imus history. The gang who gives up its mornings to sit in front of a CRT to type, the Imus on MSNBC chatter, including the great hosts Chas and Joe, kept me based in reality and gave me ideas, too, even if they were unaware of doing so.

Many thanks go to my agent, Kay Hamilton, and my editor, Jim Ellison. Ellison came up with this crazy idea for a book and picked me to write it for the Carol Publishing Group. Kay knew just the right times to encourage me and when to knock me in the head and get me cracking. I appreciate the fact that both were willing to take a chance on a first-time author like me.

Thanks to my coworkers and bosses at KSN as well. They worked with me on my schedule and covered for me when I needed it so I could find the time to go to the library or on another road trip. Special kudos to Stephanie, Mark, John, George, Heather, Jerry, and Michelene, the early morning crew, as well as Buzz, Shirley, and especially, Mike Cooper.

Thanks to my family, too, my sister Kate, who seemed to enjoy being a research assistant; Mom, who refreshed my memory; and Dad, who got me interested in Imus in the first place.

# INTRODUCTION

As I sit here and begin writing this book, I have to admit that I'm worried about attracting the wrath of the I-Man. With good reason, I believe. After all, I just watched him rant on all morning about a *Connecticut Post* article concerning his taxes that he claims was ambush journalism. He threatened to expose the writer and editors personally. That's really not what this book is about, though. What you are about to read was written by an Imus fan. I make no secret of the fact that I own both his books, I have eaten his chips, seen him in concert, and even have a denim work shirt from the Auto Body Express.

What I have tried to do here is bring a lot of people up-to-date who are just joining us. The history of Imus is a lot of fun for those of us who have experienced it. Every day I do research I discover new information and recall stories that bring a smile to my face. If this book does that for you, I'll be happy. I welcome your comments on the book, too. The best way is just to E-mail me at jimreed@everythingimus.com. I may even write back.

A quick message to Don himself. Please be gentle.

# PART I

# MOVIN' ON UP

## From Cradle to Cleveland, Again

# 1
## Don's Life, Now

"It's six o'clock, WFAN—New York" declares the radio newsman as a tall, lanky figure walks into the basement studio. Anchor Charles McCord rattles off the New York headlines while "the I-Man" gets settled in. He sets his personal microphone in place, the one with the silvery shine, pops a piece of Nicorette gum into his mouth, and begins to chew. He places the headphones to his ears. They resemble what you might use to watch a movie on an airplane, instead of large, clunky ones, a concession to the television cameras dangling from the ceiling. Five days a week the routine barely varies. It's the morning constitutional of an American icon, Don Imus.

For those who haven't seen him, the man may best be described as an aging cowboy, barely on the good side of sixty: cowboy boots, denim jeans, a shirt from his brother's store, and a denim jacket, meticulously embroidered with the four corners of the Southwest, are all part of his usual outfit. On occasion, a cowboy hat perched on some dusty silver hair completes the look. At other times he may wear a baseball cap with the glaring logo of Dreamworks or some other company he wants to plug. One particular morning, not long after the 1997 Super Bowl, he even wore a Wisconsin cheesehead to pacify NBC newsman Tim Russert. If someone were making the Imus story, maybe even this book, into a movie, Jack Palance would have the right stuff in the looks department, if not quite the right voice. Knowing Don, though, he would want to play himself so no one else screws up.

During the commercial break, he chats with McCord. Topics usually center on what Don has read or seen the night

3

before or, with any luck, a breaking scandal. These are rarely in-depth conversations. Those are reserved for when the on-air light blinks its red eye. Once his engineer, Lou, flips the switch, the light goes on, the program begins, and the heat is on. "It's five minutes after the hour (quack-quack), and I am Imus in the morning. You know, Charles . . ."

Don Imus begins four hours of what has been called the most influential radio show in America. When his voice is carried over the airwaves of 100 radio stations nationwide, from Bangor, Maine, to Los Angeles, California, he's not *just* a laugh on the way to work or while shaving. His comments will be scrutinized, ridiculed, debated, and talked about over water coolers, lunch tables, and in the halls of power, usually by people with a chuckle in their voice or a smile on their faces. Longtime fans of the show include the current governors of Georgia and Arkansas, to name just two. Imus was even named governor of Connecticut for a day, thanks to former governor Lowell Weicker. At one time, the list of Imus fans included President Bill Clinton. That admiration for the I-Man was lost after they had a falling out that will take a chapter of its own to tell. They are listening in the halls of the Capitol, though Don won't usually have a guest on who's only a lowly representative. Imus wants guests with "juice." He gets them, too; senators like Dodd, Kerry, Lieberman, and McCain.

The networks listen, too. NBC's Tom Brokaw and Tim Russert, as well as CBS's Mike Wallace and Dan Rather, are all on the Imus frequent-guest list, along with CNN's Jeff Greenfield. Opinion writers like the *Washington Post*'s Howard Kurtz and the *New York Times*'s Maureen Dowd and Frank Rich are big fans and drop his name occasionally. Jeffrey Katzenberg, from Dreamworks (a partnership he shares with Steven Spielberg and David Geffen), is a longtime associate of the I-Man's. Sports figures like Super Bowl champion coach Bill Parcells, rockers like Ted Nugent, authors such as Sam Tanenhaus, and Wall Street mavens like Dick Grasso (who runs the New York Stock Exchange) tune in to Don. If you sing the blues, you may find yourself on the Imus show, too. Don has played host to such legendary singers as James Taylor, Paul Simon, and B. B. King. None of them are safe, however. Clout and power have little effect on Don Imus. This is the man who once said, "The two most important things that happened in radio were Marconi invented it and I decided to talk on it."

Through the years he's announced several credos for his show. "We like to revel in the agony of others" (though this sounds like the royal "we," he does appear to be speaking for his crew as well) and "This show is about what *I* like and what *I* want to talk about."

The second statement usually comes back to support the first, reveling in the agony of others. One morning in early 1998, a little after seven, producer Bernard McGuirk cuts in to tell Imus that UN ambassador Bill Richardson canceled his appearance on the Imus show in order to appear on NBC's *Today* show. The rant is on, and Imus turns both barrels straight at the ambassador. "Here's our threat to Ambassador Richardson: Because you lied to us, we're going to attack you professionally and personally! Mostly personally!" The next day, he did just that, airing a scathing sketch attacking Richardson while the ambassador was on hold for the rescheduled interview. No mistake about it; this was vintage Imus.

However, guests who meet their obligation to appear on the show may still be subjected to the fury of an Imus assault. After ABC's Diane Sawyer appeared to promote a special, she was grilled about the then month-old Clinton "Interngate" scandal. It took just one commercial break for the tables to turn after she appeared. Her voice was still "echoing in the studio," as Bernard put it, while Don spent almost nine minutes attacking the journalist. (Yes, I timed it.) At the very least he called her a phony; at the most extreme, he attacked her journalistic integrity. Don, who does not suffer fools at all, let alone lightly, ranted on and on, saying she went easy on the president, possibly because she did not want to jeopardize White House access for herself and her husband, film director Mike Nichols.

One aspect of this radio-television morning show Don is true about is that he fills the program with things that interest him. A case in point is that of the Whittaker Chambers/Alger Hiss story of their long-running feud. For weeks Don became obsessed with the tale, reliving the Cuban Missile Crisis and the legends surrounding the two men. Don's young wife, Deirdre, even bought him a Hiss-style typewriter for Christmas. I-Man fans revolted. Hiss and Chambers were the last subject listeners wanted to hear discussed *every* morning on their way to work. The weeks-long ordeal came to a head one winter morning. Watching on MSNBC, you could see the anguish in Charles McCord's eyes as Imus went on and on with *another* interview of author Sam Tanenhaus, even after Chuck begged him to keep it to two questions and outright verbally attacked him when he asked his fourth. Once Don finished quizzing the scribe, Charles turned on Don like a wounded animal. "The Case is OVER! Alger Hiss is DEAD! Whittaker Chambers is DEAD! I wish I were DEAD!" While the Chambers story still surfaces occasionally, McCord seems to have put a cork in that bottle for a while.

Imus hasn't always toyed with the power players. However, politics has played a large role in his show from its beginning. When Don's radio career started, in California in 1968, one of his first gags was to run for Congress. By the end of 1971, he would become Major Market Radio Personality of the Year and be entering one of the sacred halls of broadcasting, NBC Headquarters, at 30 Rockefeller Plaza in New York. Over-the-top portrayals of a preacher by the name of Billy Sol Hargus would laugh New Yorkers awake every morning, if the screaming "WAKE UP!" didn't rattle them first. Billy Sol still shows up occasionally, though rarely now. Imus's NBC ride would last over fifteen years as a DJ, spinning records. He has made the road smooth for current "shock jocks." Howard Stern, to name one, owes much of his success to the path Imus paved for him, whether he acknowledges it or not.

In 1988, Imus began a metamorphasis. Part of the change came about as a natural extension of what was happening around him. After all, he was moving to sports radio, and records don't have much of a place there. Finally giving up drugs and booze helped. Imus abandoned the turntable and decided to go all talk, not that he was playing many records toward the end, anyway. A revived, new-style *Imus in the Morning* program began. By mid-1993 his show was syndicated out of New York into places like Boston and Washington, D.C.

With national reach comes national attention. Three times before the 1992 presidential election, the democratic hopeful, Bill Clinton, appeared on the Imus program and had a laugh with the host. After Clinton's win, Imus was truly "in the loop."

Don was even privileged to get some White House exclusives. Of course, that was before he was invited to be the speaker at the White House Radio-Television Correspondents Association's dinner. After that debacle, the pipeline to the Oval Office dried up, but Imus experienced a major growth spurt of new radio affiliates.

In 1997, *Time* magazine, for the second year in a row, came out with its list of the 25 Most Influential People in America, supposedly those with the most influence over society. That year, Imus made the list. *Time,* to accompany the one-page story, chose a photograph that was not the most flattering of Imus. It showed him in an orange jumpsuit that made him look like a member of the punk band DEVO. Being named to this list, though, seemed to mean more to Imus than his Marconi Awards for Broadcasting Excellence or his induction into the Emerson Radio Hall for Fame. This was power. Now the I-Man had "the juice." A few days after the issue came out, Imus dropped in on his friend Larry King's CNN show and proceeded to berate King over the fact that HE was on the list but King wasn't. King's lame comeback was that he "belonged on the international list."

Imus has always incorporated tongue-in-cheek humor into his show. Today, though, his cast of characters makes politics a little easier on the ear for the average American. Unlike the Sunday-morning news shows, Imus makes politics funny. His team has no problem coming up with song parodies, like Bill and Hillary Clinton singing the song "I Got a Few Babes" to the tune of Sonny and Cher's "I've Got You Babe." As long as there are people in power, Imus will have someone to attack, such as billionaire Bill Gates. Imus likes to remind listeners that he makes more money from MSNBC than the Microsoft chairman does.

Imus brings people back from the dead to tell his tales. This isn't as sick as it sounds. In taped pieces for the show, usually written by Charles McCord and performed by the talented Larry Kenney and Rob Bartlett, former president Richard Nixon provides commentary, looking through the "Dick Scope," if you will. Or Gen. George S. Patton might elaborate on the latest military options in the Imus wars. Of course, Don is not above having a few living voices created for the show, too. In addition to hearing things like the "Bill Clinton Diaries," with Bill narrating his daily whine into his journal, Paul Harvey, Rush Limbaugh, and even New York disc jockey Scott Muni (the sixth Beatle?) will offer their opinions on the air, parody style. In a bow to religion, John Cardinal O'Connor is relegated to reading the New York State Lotto numbers.

Imus has branched out, though. In 1997 he published a bestselling book, coauthored by his brother, Fred. *Two Guys, Four Corners* had people lining up for, as it is described on the show, "a hideous picture book full of rocks." All right, so it had some dirty captions. A *lot* of dirty captions. The pictures were still beautiful—Southwest photographs in the tradition of Ansel Adams with beautiful painted deserts. This "kind of autobiographical" coffee-table book will have a sequel. It deserves to, having reached the Top Twenty on *Publishers Weekly*'s bestseller list. At last check it reportedly had undergone three printings, for a total of 130,000 copies. The Imus brothers did a major autograph tour to promote the book, signing their names thirty thousand times. You could tell that the book tour was taking its toll on the brothers when their crankier-than-usual attitude was directed toward the fans in line. After waiting in line over an hour, one patron had to goad the brothers into inscribing a short birthday wish in a copy. It was nice of mom.

Imus has even played the role of proud papa. He added a baby brother to the four daughters from his first marriage in mid-1998 when second wife, Deirdre, gave birth. Fredric Wyatt Imus is over thirty years younger than his closest sister, and Don is experiencing the "joys" of having a young child in his house all over again. Though he may not remember the first era very well, he's having a lot of fun now.

After thirty years, the *Imus in the Morning* program has become must-listen radio for over 15 million people. Now sit back and try to understand how a former U.S. Marine and uranium miner got the ear of a U.S. president. Find out what a toll drugs took on his career and personal life and what battles he would have to fight along the way. Meet the people who helped make him a star, and those who help keep him fresh and funny every morning. It's more information on Imus than was ever gathered in one place before. Try not to be overwhelmed.

# ADVICE FOR WYATT

- Don't go play with sheep with your uncle Fred.

- Dad is old, and he forgets things, so if he says no, ask again in an hour.

- Mom is young and likes vegetables, but there are other kinds of food.

- Dad will share hot dogs with you when Mom is not around.

- If Dad ever gives you a hard time about doing poorly, asking him, "Will I get sent to Cleveland?" will probably shut him up.

- Asking him, "How come my sisters are older than Mommy?" will probably earn you a spanking.

# 2
## THE ROAD TO NEW YORK

He was born John Donald Imus Jr. on July 23, 1940, in Riverside, California, a city about sixty miles east of Los Angeles. His mother, Frances (maiden name, Moore) was already thirty years old when she gave birth to Don. His father, John senior, was thirty-six. The young Imus's birth date places him right on the cusp of being a Leo. That's the sign of the lion (the king of the jungle) and a fire and energy sign, if you believe in horoscopes. Two years later, Frances and John senior would give birth to Fredric, or Fred, as he's more commonly known.

The family business was ranching, and it was a good one for the Imus family in the forties. Don and Fred grew up on a 35,000-acre ranch he's called the Willows in Prescott, Arizona, about halfway between Phoenix and Flagstaff, though a little off the beaten path. So much so that the highway seems to pass near Prescott rather than through it on the map.

Don's life as a younger child is hard to recount, mostly because he doesn't spend much time talking about it. He does say that he could ride a horse before he could lead it back to the stables. Mostly, Don fondly speaks of summers on the ranch as some of the best times of his life. Just one of his inspirations to begin his Imus Ranch Foundation. Living on a remote ranch in Arizona gave Don ample time to listen to the radio. He would take his transistor and tune in a high-powered station from Mexico that broadcast a steady diet of preachers hawking Jesus and Wolfman Jack playing the latest hits, both of whom would inspire him when he launched his career in radio years later. So would his family; his mother and father

10

both had a sense of humor. No surprise when you look at their boys now.

Don has mentioned that both he and Fred spent time in private schools when they were young. Later, though, Don ended up attending the public Scottsdale High School in a suburb of Phoenix, where trouble was never far behind. He told of being arrested in Phoenix after a school fight and once told *New York* magazine that he was elected eighth-grade class president and then impeached. Obviously he was a rebel early on.

He became interested in music in high school. Imus the singer was joined by a five-piece band. His job would be to sing like Fats Domino—hits like "Yes It's Me" and "I'm in Love Again." He was influenced by singers like Fats, Bo Diddley, Little Richard, and Hank Ballard and the Midnighters.

Divorce would split up the family when Don was just fifteen years old, something a lot less common in 1955 than today. It was only a couple of years later that Don would drop out of high school and find himself in uniform.

In the years between World War II and Vietnam, the military was the place to get an education and a steady job. It was 1957, and John Donald Imus Jr., just seventeen, enlisted in the U.S. Marine Corps. Since he lived west of the Mississippi, Imus went to "Hollywood" boot camp near San Diego instead of Parris Island. Imus told Murray the K in a later interview that his mother pushed him into joining to keep him out of jail.

After boot camp, Imus took the role of a performer-soldier. He became a bugler in the Marine Corps band at California's Camp Pendleton, just north of San Diego. Imus eventually reached the rank of private first class. The Parris Island Marine Museum showcases a small display of Imus as one of many famous Americans who served their country in the corps.

The "Marines' Hymn" refers to the halls of Montezuma and the shores of Tripoli, but it never mentions Tijuana. That's the part of the world marine Imus wanted to see, though. He ventured off base one day, minus a pass, to take a trip south of the border, just a short ride from San Diego. Don admitted, "There was only one reason to go to Tijuana at the time."

We'll let the city's reputation speak for itself. Unfortunately for the frustrated young I-Man, he was stopped at the border. He doesn't remember whether it was a lack of proper papers, like a pass or driver's license, or his age that kept him in the United States, but he does remember the result. The border patrol called his parents.

Imus did two years in the marine band and apparently inspired his brother, because Fred enlisted in the U.S. Army. According to Fred, he was one of the elite paratroopers in the 101st Airborne Division. Suffice it to say that a hard landing or two might just explain why Fred is not all there some days.

Postmarine life became a difficult transition for Don. His goal was to be in a band, so he gravitated to Los Angeles and Southern California during that time. He took some odd jobs to pay the bills, including a job as a window dresser in San Bernardino. His job was to set up displays in department-store windows and dress the mannequins. What he did, though, was stage mock stripteases for the life-sized wooden figures; it would be one of many times he was fired from a job.

These were not easy times to try breaking into music. Don spent some time homeless, admitting to having slept behind the dryers in a laundromat and scaring the poor women who found him there. He spent time in jail for writing checks that didn't always clear. He had some trouble with not paying a few tickets, too. He did backbreaking work, like mining for uranium and copper in Arizona's Grand Canyon. He never seemed to let up trying to make his way with a career in music, though.

After the washout with the window dressing, the Imus brothers headed to Hollywood, where they did have some minor success. Under the names Jay Jay Imus (Don) and his partner, Freddie Ford (Fred), they published a record on the Challenge label called "I'm a Hot Rodder, and All That Jazz." In fact, an older picture Don recently shared with the world on MSNBC shows him dressed as a crooner, in late-fifties style, posed behind a microphone in a suit, white shirt, thin tie, and a hat that makes him look like a young Eliot Ness. He also recorded tunes on the RV and Delphi labels.

His family life in the sixties took many great turns, but involved problems most people in their twenties deal with. Most tragic was dealing with the loss of his father. John Donald

Imus Sr. died in 1962, just fifty-eight years old, and never saw the future success of his namesake son. Imus would also take a bride. He walked down the aisle with Harriet, who would end up following him across the country while he searched for his niche in life. Children followed, too, both in the sense of time and travel. By the end of the sixties there would be four of them: Nadine, Toni, Elizabeth, and Ashleigh.

He did find a better way after a while. He began working as a brakeman for the Southern Pacific Railroad, switching box-cars in Oxnard. He's glad to tell you about it on the radio, too. Compared to the mines it was easy work. It was also the six-ties; one could drink or smoke while working. The part of the story you probably won't hear Imus mention on the radio is why he left the railroad in 1966. A train wreck left him with a severely injured back and eventually a cash settlement from the railroad.

Don, out of a job with the railroad, wanted to return to music. Of course, the best way to be successful in the music industry is to get your songs played on the radio. So he came up with a plan. Back in the mid-sixties, there was a little thing called "payola," giving the deejay a "bonus" for playing your record. The better the bonus payment, the more often it was played or the higher it was rated. Around that time you could buy some decent air play for fifty dollars. The main problem was that it was illegal, and the Federal Communications Com-mission (FCC) eventually cracked down on the practice. At the time, though, Don figured the best way to beat the system was to become a disk jockey and play the records that he and Fred were making. (As a side note, Don says he still owes a couple of plays to Fleetwood Mac.)

Imus enrolled at the Don Martin School of Broadcasting in Hollywood. FCC rules being what they were back in the six-ties, you needed a license to operate the station if you were a deejay. So Imus took the classes he needed and got the license. He didn't get his diploma, however. It seems he was five hun-dred dollars short when it came time to make the last payment to the Don Martin School. He would eventually pay up after making it big and get his diploma.

Sheepskin or not, Imus was armed with the legal paperwork he needed in 1968 and was ready to break into radio. So he headed to Palmdale, California, a small town about thirty miles south of Edwards Air Force base. Imus arrived on the doorstep of 1470 AM KUTY, a 5,000-watt station, small by most standards. The Imus radio career would officially start on June 1, 1968. In 1996 the *Antelope Valley Press* took a look back at their favorite son and found that Art Furtado was the station manager at KUTY when Imus arrived. Even back then his station manager realized that Don was a tremendous talent. To the station's owners hiring Imus wasn't much more of an investment, so Imus could do pretty much what he wanted.

His pay at the time was about eighty dollars a week. Not bad for a fledgling disk jockey in the Antelope Valley of California, northeast of Los Angeles. The paltry sum was not enough for the I-Man, though. He had his sights set on politics even then. Congressmen made over forty thousand dollars a year in those days. So Don Imus, an Independent, attempted to knock off Barry Goldwater Jr. for the right to represent the greater Palmdale area in Washington. Imus actually garnered a few hundred votes.

While Imus was enjoying his job, he didn't have much intention of staying in radio. After all, he wanted to get those records played and have that big music career he still aspired to. Since he felt that he had a good sense of timing, his tenure at KUTY didn't last very much longer. After only eight months on the air, he moved his radio career one step up the ladder by moving on to Stockton, California's KJOY.

The move to Stockton made Imus some pretty good money. He was now pulling down about eight hundred dollars a month, more than double his Palmdale salary. The outrageousness didn't stop, though. He conducted an Eldridge Cleaver look-alike contest. The prize—money or jail time if you looked like the fugitive Black Panther leader. The contest had both good and bad results; he was fired after ten months but stumbled across a man who would greatly help his career.

After looking around for work, Don ended up in Sacramento, California, and met general manager of KXOA, Jack G. Thayer. Thayer was working his way toward becoming a big name in broadcasting by pioneering the idea of talk radio.

Thayer, Imus was told, was probably the only man who would hire him. Imus credits Jack Thayer with inspiring him to develop characters. Thayer didn't actually come up with them but he pointed out that by using characters Imus could continue to skewer what was happening in the world, but a little less controversially. Among the first group of Imus's made-up merry men were a southern radio preacher named "the Right Reverend Dr. Billy Sol Hargus" and a perverted storyteller named "Crazy Bob."

Hargus was the world's most outrageous evangelist. Lampooning a trade that has given us people like Jimmy Swaggert, who lost his glory by favoring prostitutes, and Jim Bakker, who lost his ministry by embezzling millions, was easy for anyone. Imus did it years earlier and made it an art form.

Hargus's home church was the First Church of the Gooey Death and Discount House of Worship in Del Rio, Texas. From there, you could mail-order just about any piece of crap you could think of, according to Imus. Hargus sold everything, from sacred chickens to Jesus statues for your dashboard. He was a walking scam, of course. After all, you didn't really *buy* anything, you just got it for a prayer offering. It was those preachers Imus listened to as a kid on Mexican radio who inspired him.

Crazy Bob, on the other hand, was just a demented pervert. The boy just wasn't right and told truly twisted fairy tales peppered with pop-culture references, kind of like Mr. Rogers as done by Marilyn Manson. Imagine Goldilocks in bed with Baby Bear or Mary Poppins keeping the kids calm through the power of home-style pharmacology.

It was also in Sacramento that Imus came up with one of the comedy bits that he still plays snippets of today. It's called "1,200 Hamburgers," and it's still a classic. Imus was one of the first phone freaks, just as the Jerky Boys were to the early nineties, calling out and harassing people in their homes and businesses and putting them on the air. This prank starts with a call to MacDonald's and Imus launching into the poor squeaky-voiced boy who answers the phone. He identifies himself as "Sergeant Kirkland of the Air National Guard," and he is in need of twelve hundred hamburgers for troops on maneu-

## Hargus Merchandise

Here are just a few of the items you might have been able to buy for a prayer donation from Reverend Hargus's First Church of the Gooey Death and Discount House of Worship in Del Rio, Texas. Remember, all are available "for a limited time and a limited time only!"

- A Plastic Dashboard Jesus: His eyes light up when you hit your brake lights.

- The First National Bank of Him: You *can* take it with you to heaven.

- Holyland Record Package: $3.98

- Real Estate in Heaven: $5,000 will reserve a detached bungalow.

- Blank Bibles: Swear anything you want on them.

- Sacred Chickens: So holy they won't soil your dishes

- "Hittin' Them Hotlicks With Him" book: music lessons, to play in the band with Jesus.

vers. The phone voice panics, worried that he doesn't have enough buns! That's not the least of his problems, though, because Imus has a special order. Three hundred with ketchup but no mustard, one hundred of those with no onions, etc. This bit would eventually lead off Don's first comedy album, called *1,200 Hamburgers to Go.*

Imus seemed to love the telephone for his bits. In addition to taking calls from listeners, he would make random calls to homes. "Are you naked?" he would ask female callers once they answered the phone, not knowing who was on the other end.

The telephone would attract attention to Imus from a totally different group, the FCC, the governmental entity that regulates the telephones and, more important, the airwaves of America. They set the rules for decency, like the seven words you can't say on television (or the radio). The mass-media bureau assigns frequencies to television and radio stations, approves sales of stations, and performs other administrative tasks. Because of phone pranks by deejays, the FCC put a law on the books in 1970 to stop the practice. Imus was more than happy to take credit for the rule, which appears in Section 73 of the federal code:

> Title 47 Code of Federal Regulations, SS 73 § 73.1206 Broadcast of telephone conversations.
>
> Before recording a telephone conversation for broadcast, or broadcasting such a conversation simultaneously with its occurrence, a licensee shall inform any party to the call of the licensee's intention to broadcast the conversation, except where such party is aware, or may be presumed to be aware from the circumstances of the conversation, that it is being or likely will be broadcast. Such awareness is presumed to exist only when the other party to the call is associated with the station (such as an employee or part-time reporter), or where the other party originates the call and it is obvious that it is in connection with a program in which the station customarily broadcasts telephone conversations. [35 FR 7733, May 20, 1970]

While he might have had some input in its passage and want to take credit for it, nowhere in the proposed law is there a mention of Don Imus. It's pretty fair to say he contributed something to the controversy, though.

FCC or not, Imus was attracting attention. In 1969, *Billboard* magazine named him the Medium Market Disc Jockey of the Year for his work at KXOA.

Running a successful radio station often attracts attention, too. It allows you other opportunities to run radio stations, and that was true for Jack Thayer. When Don's new mentor headed off to Cleveland, Don Imus soon followed. The station was WGAR, what is now called a CHR station, which is contemporary hit radio, or Top Forty. The station was owned by the big corporate entity Nationwide Insurance. Nationwide paid well, too, reportedly sixteen thousand dollars a year for the I-Man's services.

Boss Radio is how it was described, with a wall of sound, music everywhere, shotgun jingles, and more. The I-Man even had custom jingles of his own. One shouted "The Best of Imus," followed in true Imus fashion by the singers breaking up and asking, "Who's Imus?"

While in Cleveland, Imus was gaining national acclaim. In the early 1970s several albums were released featuring some of the up-and-coming disc jockeys of the time. Among those included were Charlie Tuna, on KROQ in Los Angeles, and Scott Shannon, on WMAK in Chicago. Tuna would go on to become probably the premier voice-over announcer on television. He worked for everyone, from major television shows (including being the announcer on NBC's *Scrabble*) to being the news voice of numerous television stations across the country and one of Rick Dees's predecessors on KIIS in Los Angeles. Shannon would go on to compete against Imus more than once in New York, and they would even work together.

The featured clip was great for a laugh, and a look at the Imus psyche. On the recording, Don is conversing with a producer of *The Dating Game*, trying to work his way in as a contestant. He dodges the question of whether he is married. (We're pretty sure he was at the time.) The questioning then turns to affiliation; the producer wants to know if it is any prob-

# SYNDICATION MILESTONES

1973–74   Imus and Wolfman Jack host a national radio New Year's Eve broadcast.

1980s   Imus is carried as fill on NBC Radio network, not for broadcast, but it made plenty of board operators around the country Imus fans!

June/93   WQYK Tampa

July/93   WEEI Boston, WWRX Providence, and WTEM Washington, D.C.

July/94   one-year anniversary, Imus on thirty affiliates

May/96   Imus "Trailer Park Tour" to Raleigh; Branson, Missouri; and Wichita, Kansas

July/96   KLAC Los Angeles, WYST Detroit, and WGMP Philadelphia join.

September/96   KPIX San Francisco joins.

1998   Imus heard on 104 radio stations across the country.

lem that *The Dating Game* appears on ABC. In true Imus style, he tells her there is no conflict, because while he is on NBC, that doesn't matter, because "I don't pay any attention to that. I've got three Jew attorneys in New York that can put anybody on their knees."

When the producer offers to talk off the air, Imus pronounces one of the mottoes he has kept to this day. "My policy in the four years I've been in radio is to do what I want and if they don't like it, they can get somebody else, Jack."

Imus's "do what I want" attitude was pervasive through his time in Cleveland (and even today). The problems really started creeping in, though. A writer for the *Cleveland Plain Dealer* caught Imus's show and was not impressed. In fact, he was so disgusted that he encouraged a protest of the Imus show. He told all Nationwide policyholders to voice their opinions of Imus by sending their insurance policies back to the company. Apparently, the business loss was not great, for Imus confirms on the air how great Nationwide Insurance was to stand behind him.

It paid off for Imus and Nationwide. In 1971 the music-industry publication *Billboard* named Don Imus the Major Market Personality of the Year. This is surprising for a couple of reasons. One, the award has always gone to a New York or Los Angeles deejay, someone from a major market. However, they knew a star when they spotted one in Don Imus. The other surprise is Imus's relative inexperience. Despite encouragement and coaching, Imus was on his fourth radio job in three years. His resume was not exactly similar to those of other radio stars around that time, like Wolfman Jack and Robert W. Morgan.

Imus would move on to a fifth job before the end of his fifth year in broadcasting. Like a record that rockets to the top of the charts, the I-Man rocketed to the top of the radio world. In the summer of 1971, Don Imus was called up to the big leagues of radio.

# 3
...
# WELCOME TO 30 ROCK

**R**ockefeller Center and Rockefeller Plaza are two of New York's most prestigious historical landmarks. Featuring the famous Radio City Music Hall, the ice-skating rink, the now defunct Rainbow Room, and every holiday season, the giant Christmas tree, the location is instantly identifiable. Anchoring it all is a towering skyscraper that boasts the street address 30 Rockefeller Plaza. Called by various names throughout the years, including the RCA Building and now the GE Building, since the 1920s the tower has been home to the studios and offices of the world headquarters of the National Broadcasting Company, or NBC.

In the early 1970s the second floor was the home of the flagship, or premier, station of the National Broadcasting Company, WNBC in New York, the radio in Radio City. The station had once welcomed satirists Bob and Ray and Bill Cullen as their morning-show hosts and had broadcast live concerts across the nation from their studios. WNBC was the home of many firsts in broadcasting in its fifty-year history: the first commercial broadcast, the first presidential broadcast, and the first network-sponsored broadcast. It was such a powerful station, it was once received in South Africa, over seven thousand miles away.

In the early seventies 66 WNBC AM and 97.1 WNBC FM simulcast a "full service" format, best described as Top Forty music, and news at the top and bottom of the hour. They were regarded at the time as also-rans in the radio market, behind 77 WABC. On December 2, 1971, the man whom people in Palmdale had first heard as Captain Don four years earlier sat down

21

behind the microphone. Welcome to New York, *Imus in the Morning.*

Imus's schedule, like that of many deejays today, called for him to work the morning shift, 6–10 A.M., six days a week. That first day must have really stressed him out, because he didn't make it in the next morning for his air shift. It was the first of many he would miss.

The show was similar to what he had been doing in Cleveland. Music, taped comedy bits, and phone calls filled four hours of airtime. Imus took his well-developed characters, like the Right Reverend Dr. Billy Sol Hargus and Crazy Bob, and expanded them to new heights for his new audience. His pack of parodists included some even more outrageous people as well. "Judge Hangin'" came on the scene as a true southern judge who thought hanging was actually getting off easy. Tinsel town was represented by a lisper named "Hy from Hollywood," and "Brother Love" advised the women in his congregation on affairs of the heart. While all of the above are retired now, one of his early bits lives on today in the David Brinkley–sounding "Imus in Washington." That makes it almost thirty years old and still running.

A man who was an early Imus fan, and continues to be to this day, is Jack Schnapper. Schnapper is a former programmer for the Sperry Corporation and now owner of his own Internet design business, which includes a fantastic *Imus in the Morning* page, one of the most popular on the Net. Jack made a stop at 30 Rock one day in the early seventies just to meet Imus and even made it past security to Don's secretary. He and a friend were autograph hunting and were not disappointed. After some lighthearted harassing by Imus, both walked away with the I-Man's signature.

Schnapper had Imus fortune shine on him again in the early seventies. That Imus had to put on six shows a week doesn't mean he actually had to get up on Saturday mornings. There was a lot of pressure on Imus, but despite that, he was a perfectionist about his show and still is. The Saturday-morning shows were taped during the week, and Schnapper found his way into the engineer's studio during one of the tapings. Imus didn't actually have to run his own controls and probably

# DISGRUNTLED SPONSORS

- Irish Airlines: Imus warned that Protestants had to ride coach.

- Carvel Ice Cream: Rob Bartlett as Tom Carvel—'nuff said?

- Donald Trump: On and off, Imus has trashed the hotels; Trump has pulled his ads.

- Chrysler: Cars named after a letter (like K) spell disaster.

couldn't, due to union rules, so he sat behind the glass and spewed into the microphone while the engineer lorded over the dials. The engineer took it on the chin, though, over his music selection. After one transition, according to Schnapper, the down-to-earth Imus gave a few hints to the engineer. The I-Man's music strategy was simple: "You never play two upbeat songs back-to-back, you never play two slow songs back-to-back, and you never play two niggers back-to-back."

That was nothing compared to what he said on the air. It wasn't long before Imus was offending sponsors. A favorite story concerns an Irish Airlines live commercial he had to read. He launched into the spot and at the end noted, "Protestants have to ride coach." WNBC lost the account.

He teamed up with famous comedians, too. Lily Tomlin did a bit on the show as a little girl engaged in conversation with a dirty old man (Imus). He offers her candy; she asks for Rolaids. After all, that's what old people like him are supposed to have, and besides, she needs something to wash down the hamster sandwich. The bit lasted less than ninety seconds, but it's hilarious.

It was around this time that the duck came along as well. Now, anyone who has listened to Imus for more than a few minutes has probably heard the "quack-quack" of a duck. The story is actually pretty simple when Imus tells it. It seems that in the early days at WNBC he had an engineer with him who had a short attention span. So short that while Imus was ranting on, he would become distracted and miss cues for songs and breaks. Imus, Mr. Perfectionist when it comes to the sound of the show, instituted the duck. Whenever he would give the time, the engineer was to play the "quack-quack" duck sound. Just that simple, but it made him listen. It's been part of the show at times and gone away at others, but as of today, the duck survives.

Imus attracted the attention of *Life* magazine in November 1972. They featured a big spread on the morning show host, appropriately entitled "I'm Imus, and I'm the Best." It was an easy claim to make for the public Imus, whose ego seemed in overdrive, but somewhat justified with two Disc Jockey of the

Year Awards. The article by Richard Woodley tells of Don's first year in New York. If you've seen Imus on MSNBC, you will recognize one of the pictures from the photo spread on the back wall of the WFAN studio. It portrays the early Imus well, sunglasses on and hair flying everywhere while he cues a record.

Not long after arriving on the morning program, Don Imus was paired with a new newsman from Springfield, Missouri. This talented radio journalist had actually been working his way to New York since 1963. The two became friends and the now-infamous collaboration began with Charles McCord.

McCord has been vocal about Imus's problems in the early seventies, as well as his good sides. He has often talked about how, like a family member checking up on the hired help, he used to mark bottles of booze to monitor Imus's drinking. The absences were getting extreme: Imus missed his second day at WNBC. The newsroom reportedly had a pool going. Pick the next day Imus would miss work and you'd win a prize. Reportedly, in 1973, Imus missed over a hundred days of work.

Imus was generous with his time and money, though. In fact, McCord also tells the story of "Imus the Rich Guy." To this day, there is still not a lot of money to be made by most people in radio, but Don Imus, after starting at $425 a month in California, was making $80,000 a year to start at WNBC. That's not what Imus told people, though. He claimed his salary was in the six-figure range. Imus the Rich Guy had a special quirk, it seems. On occasion, he would walk through the lobby of the station, pull out a wad of bills, break the seal on them, and let them scatter to the floor as he walked away. A nice way to pick up a bonus.

Imus was living the high life. Don, Harriet, and their four daughters were living in a house in Greenwich, Connecticut. Imus was driving a Lincoln Mark IV and lusting after a Rolls. He was doing personal appearances and signing autographs.

He was also performing outside of radio. In early March 1973, Imus was working on a nightclub act at the Bitter End in New York's Greenwich Village. He caught the attention of a local newsman who was also on his way to becoming famous. Geraldo Rivera, then working for WABC-TV in New York, filmed some of the rehearsal and put together a three-minute-long segment about Imus to run on his station. The plan was for Geraldo to show it on *Eyewitness News*'s 6:00 P.M. report one Tuesday night. The segment was even promoted at the beginning of the program. According to the *New York Times,* however, "midway through the show, Mr. Rivera said, he was summoned from the set and told the segment had been killed because it was 'offensive.'"

Rivera returned to the set and acknowledged that the segment would not be shown. He then walked out of the station, threatening to not return over the censorship. After much talk and after editing out Imus's comments about a rival anchorman, Rivera returned, and the segment aired two days later.

After winning two of *Billboard*'s Disc Jockey of the Year Awards, in 1969 and 1970, Imus was asked to present the awards in 1972. In what may have been the first demonstration that public dinners and speeches may not be the best forum for Imus, he performed the entire program in the character of Reverend Hargus. According to the *Life* magazine report, none of the winners was even allowed to speak. It's hard to say what he was thinking at the time, though drinking may have had something to do with his behavior. Imus, while fine behind a microphone with two people across the room, was uncomfortable doing lunches with advertisers and personal appearances, so he turned to the bottle for some liquid backbone.

At the end of 1973, NBC put together two of its biggest stars for a national New Year's Eve broadcast. Imus got to work with the same man he had enjoyed listening to so many years earlier while on the ranch in Arizona. Don joined Wolfman Jack in hosting on radio a live party combined with reports from a newsman in Times Square. Imus started off by hammering Wolfman for jumping around like a fat Mexican. While interviewing party guests, he tried to pawn off a fourteen-year-old girl on the Wolfman for a kiss. With friends like Imus, right? Just after midnight, Wolfman told how he had the traditional black beans and rice. Imus said he had just eaten a kitty.

There were more strange broadcasts to come. In 1975, in addition to his regular show, Imus was tapped to fill in for Norm N. Nite. The *Nite-Train* show would play DooWop records, or was supposed to, anyway. (You can still hear Norm on WCBS-FM 101.1 in New York.) Imus hosted the Sunday-night show along with Jay Black from Jay and the Americans, a band that dished out some classic hits like "Cara Mia" and "Come a Little Bit Closer." While Jay may have enjoyed making the music that lives on today on the oldies stations, from hearing that show it's apparent that Jay did not want to be behind the microphone that night.

Imus played around in his usual style and even managed to suck Jay in to helping with a couple of live commercials. Now, live commercials were pretty popular back in the seventies, and not only was Imus good at them, he was unpredictable as hell. Nothing seemed to illustrate this better than that very night when Imus went on and on for a local air-conditioning dealer. Throughout the night, every time the ad would come up, seemingly about once an hour, Imus would update us on the repairman's travels. He ended up at some grandma's house with a goat before it was all over.

While the listeners were howling at the ads, management was less than enthusiastic. Sometime during the evening a phone call came into the control room for Imus. The sales manager of the station was not thrilled with Black's chiming in on the ads, Imus told his listeners. Imus didn't seem to like getting the call from management, however, and instead of complying, he offered a little revenge on the salesman, reminding him: "I know where the bodies are buried."

It's rare that anyone gets the best of Don Imus, but Robert W. Morgan sure did. Robert W. Morgan is another of America's famous disc jockeys, having spent time all across the country; for example, WIND in Chicago and KFI in Los Angeles. Morgan may have been to Los Angeles what Imus is to New York. While Imus has claimed a friendship with Morgan, these two stories will demonstrate that someone can get the best of Imus.

In 1973, *Billboard* asked the two jocks to submit a tape to be considered for their awards. Morgan joined Don on his show to try and produce one good reel. Morgan was attacking everyone, notably WABC's Dan Ingram and, of course, Don Imus. He told Imus that if WNBC could be heard in thirty-eight states, that meant he had four listeners a state and that Billy Sol Hargus was nothing but a Billy Graham rip-off. Imus turned on the charm of Reverend Hargus, and Morgan did one of his famous bits, which amounted to a radio baptism during which he would "Morganize" a woman. As the pair progressed through the show, the more Imus would try to talk, the more Morgan would attempt to take him down. Morgan eventually got the last laugh, though. Imus had to close the program over the telephone. Morgan stole all the microphones in the studio and had headed out of the building.

On another occasion, Morgan called Imus and informed him that he was about to receive the Broadcaster of the Year Award. Imus was ready to accept. So ready that he headed straight for New Orleans. Only when he arrived did he find out. It was all a Morgan practical joke; no award for the I-Man this time.

Things were changing at WNBC, though. Through the sixties and early seventies, FM broadcasting was just an addition to that of AM for most stations, another way to get the signal out. In 1975, WNBC decided to make more of an effort (or shall we say, profit) on FM. On June 18, 1975, WNBC-FM became WNWS-FM. While on the AM side the format remained music and Imus, WNWS-FM became the flagship of NBC's all-news radio network, headed by Jack Thayer. Thirty-three stations signed on for the first broadcast, which was actually covered by NBC-TV's *Today* show.

There was still more change in the air, though. Imus's "army" of advertisers, as they were called, was a loyal group of sponsors behind the show. Even with them, however, there were reports that the station was losing close to $1.5 million a year, an astronomical figure in 1976. Ratings performance was poor, too. The station that could reach thirty-eight states at night with one of the most powerful signals in the area finished seventeenth out of forty-five broadcasters rated.

In June 1977 the corporate heads of NBC Radio could wait

for a change no longer. A management change was made; the station manager and program director were fired. The new team was imported from Chicago, though the pair had originally joined forces in Pittsburgh. NBC corporate headquarters appointed Charlie Warner WNBC's general manager, and his protégé, twenty-three-year-old Bob Pittman, was named program director, and thus Imus's direct boss. Pittman and Warner were apparently well regarded in the NBC corporate structure for turning around Chicago's WMAK radio, which had gone from fifteenth to third. They faced a much bigger challenge at WNBC, but they had an idea for a change.

# 4

# RISING FROM THE ASHES

The announcement was made on a day in late August 1977. The *New York Times* headline said it all: "WNBC Radio Shifts Cast and Policy." New management at WNBC, led by Bob Pittman, decided to change formats. High-profile-personality radio was out, and music was in. On September 1 a Who's Who list of New York disc jockeys was replaced in one fell swoop. Seasoned announcers like Cousin Brucie Morrow, Walt Baby Love, and Don Imus were out.

The format changed, too. The idea was similar to one heard even today on radio stations around the country: "less talk, more music." While a report in *New York* magazine said that the station even considered going to an all-disco format, this was rejected in favor of the Top Forty music the station was already competing with.

The change was probably the most drastic in the mornings. For six years, New Yorkers had been waking up with Imus and his cast of characters. The change Pittman and Warner made to replace Imus was to bring in someone handpicked from within the NBC family. Ellie Dyland made the jump to New York from Chicago to fill the 6–10 A.M. time period. A spokeswoman quoted in the *New York Times* said, "She will be the only morning 'man' on AM radio in the entire country who's a woman."

Meanwhile, "God's Chosen Disc Jockey" was out of work and at what had to be one of the lowest points in his life to date. Drinking and drugs were taking their toll on the thirty-seven-year-old man. Friends and family mostly watched from the sidelines, witnessing Imus's self-destruction. He was now out of work and without Charles McCord, his friend and writer, who had been spared from the sweeping changes on the programming side of WNBC.

Imus had a deal in New York when he left NBC. He was wooed by Metromedia television to do a syndicated talk show. *Imus Plus* premiered on WNEW-TV in New York and was a failure. Don could at least take credit that he beat his buddy Geraldo Rivera to the talk-show circuit.

When television didn't work out, Imus would step backward one rung on his career ladder. He would head back to the shores of Lake Erie, in Cleveland, Ohio. This time the station was WHK in Cleveland, which was actually a Metromedia radio station. He relocated Harriet and his four daughters and started polishing up his act again. Many accounts considered the move "banishment" to Cleveland, but that does not seem to be the case.

Whereas getting to New York had to be one of the best of times, no doubt returning to Cleveland was one of the worst. That is saying a lot for a guy who had been through train accidents and the loss of his father, even if change seems to be a constant in the broadcasting industry. It was a friend who really set him straight, according to a 1994 *Esquire* interview with Martha Sherrill: "My lawyer, Michael Lynne, was one of the few people who was straight with me. When I got fired, he told me, 'I don't think you really have the guts to straighten yourself out. I think you're fucked up.' Everybody else told me I'd be okay." Perhaps a resolve to prove Lynne wrong was the biggest reason for Don to clean up his act.

There exists a strange relationship between radio in the city of Cleveland and that in New York City. Cleveland has to be some sort of breeding ground. An incubator, if you will. It lets broadcasters grow and bloom before sending them out of the hothouse and into the fire. It happened for Imus in 1971, and it happened to others. Larry Kenney spent time at Cleveland's WKYC, and one of the biggest names ever in radio made his way in Cleveland—Alan Freed, who coined the term "rock 'n' roll." Imus may have even bumped into Al Roker, who also spent time at WKYC in 1978. Even Cleveland businessmen have made it big in New York. George Steinbrenner bought the Yankees for less than $10 million and now has a team that is probably worth over $400 million.

During afternoons at WHK, Imus's life was probably drab and unexciting when compared to where he had just come from. He was living in a subdivision far removed from Greenwich and Park Avenue. His act was improving, though, and he was cleaning his life up as well. On the air Imus was still capable of being an attack dog. When he heard that the president of Cleveland's city council, George Forbes, got off on a bribery charge because he took the money but apparently didn't do anything for it, he called and congratulated him. He told him that if he, Forbes, had been Ted Kennedy at Chappaquidick, he probably would have reported the car stolen.

By the way, wondering why so many references to Kennedy, even today? Well, that may be because of Imus's literary agent Esther "Lobster" Newberg. Newberg was a roommate of Mary Joe Kopechne's, who died in the Chappaquidick-bridge car accident. She later went on to work on books with the Kennedys.

Meanwhile, back in New York, the growth Pittman had attempted to stimulate at WNBC had not been as spectacular as that in Chicago. Less than a year after its start, the "morning man . . . who's a woman" project would end. Ellie Dyland was out, and by the end of 1978, all but three of the new disc jockeys brought in during the September 1977 clean sweep had left the station. Of course, one of the obvious options for Bob Pittman and Charlie Warner was to bring Imus back from Cleveland. Instead, the management chose to handpick a team and build their own morning show.

The first member of the team was a career disc jockey named Scotty Brink. Brink had been spinning records since he was seventeen and, by the time he reached NBC, had over twenty years in the business. He spent time leading the nomadic life of a disc jockey, climbing up the ladder in Williamsport, Pennsylvania, Chicago, Philly, and even in New York under the name J. J. Jordan. On WNBC's morning show he would play the role of straight man.

His partner, on the other hand, according to a *New York* magazine article, had never even been in a radio studio until he signed his deal with WNBC. He was a thirty-four-year-old stand-up comedian named Richard Belzer. Originally, Belzer was a contributor, providing a couple of bits three times a week while he worked stand-up in Manhattan's comedy clubs. He was eventually bumped up to two hours a day, from 7 to 9 A.M.

The new team was promoted heavily. Television ads blanketed the city, and articles like the one in *New York* didn't hurt. What might have hurt, though, were the constant comparisons to Don Imus. It was almost as if his ghost still occupied the studio. The *New York* article devoted three full pages of text to the morning pair at a time slot that author Scot Haller described as "the crucial morning slot on the prestigious flagship station of a 282-station network." The article also spent considerable space comparing the two to Imus. Don is mentioned no less than six times in the piece by name, and Haller criticizes Brink and Belzer for apparently not being as funny: "They have yet to produce a classic moment to rival Imus's ordering 1,200 hamburgers to go. . . ."

Before the end of the article it is mentioned that Brink and Belzer both had three-year deals with the station. They wouldn't even get through three more months. Almost two months to the day after the *New York* article on Brink and Belzer appeared, the pair was history. Where are they now? Well, Richard Belzer does his stand-up occasionally, but he is really part of the "Must-See TV" lineup at NBC. Belzer plays Det. John Munch on the acclaimed drama *Homicide, Life on the Street*. Brink is still in radio. His resumé lists over twenty stations, with the most recent being KXGL-FM in San Diego.

It appeared to be time for a new morning man on WNBC. Hearing the rumors that Imus was improving, an emissary was sent to Cleveland to check out his show. When Don, through the grapevine, heard about this apparent interest, he pulled out every decent bit he had done in Cleveland and played them all. It worked. He was welcomed back on the air at 66 WNBC. He received a substantial salary increase as well; estimates show that Imus was paid $1 million a year to return to Radio City.

On September 3, 1979, John Donald Imus Jr. probably found himself repeating the very same steps he had taken in December 1971. He headed into 30 Rock to take his place behind the console in a second-floor studio. In the early-morning hours, he settled in and tried to live up to the new pressure he must have felt. Imus was no longer a hotshot kid with three years in broadcasting and making eighty thousand dollars a year. He was now an experienced professional less than a year from turning forty. He was making a huge salary and had to show he was once again equal to the responsibility.

Imus, as "God's Chosen, Re-Rosen Disc Jockey" was back on the big 66 WNBC. Amazingly enough, he was again working for Bob Pittman, the program director who just two years before had banished him with the rest of the announcers. WNBC Radio had not been profitable since the early seventies.

While in his first incarnation he had worked with a rotating group of newsmen, Imus was now paired permanently with Charles McCord. In the early seventies, McCord was part of a group that included Jim Ire, but now it would be Imus and McCord as a team. Actually, McCord was the first person Don called with the news of his return. A good example of the partnership in action: It was the words written by Charles McCord that Don read on his first day back as Billy Sol.

McCord and Imus would team to create a silly Godzilla-like character named Moby Worm. The threat of Moby's attacking the tristate area was ever present, and so was the intrepid reporter "Captain" Frank Reed. Reed was recruited in-house. At one point he hosted the *Frank Reed All Request Radio Show* middays on WNBC. When Moby would attack (he eventually spoke, too, in the synthesized voice of Don Imus), Captain Frank would be there. If memory serves me correctly, Captain Frank, much like Kenny from South Park, would die. Frequently.

Imus said in articles as late as 1983 that he had cleaned up his act now. However, while the public Imus was basking in the glory of his return, his private life continued to be troubling. His wife, Harriet, along with his four daughters, now ranging in age from ten to seventeen years old, did not return to New York with Don. They remained in Cleveland. In the early 1980s, Don and Harriet's marriage came to an end. Imus would say later that he probably wasn't a very good father to his daughters, not having been there for much of their early lives. Don thinks Harriet would probably concur that the marriage had been an unfortunate one.

On the air, though, the show became totally revitalized. New characters popped up on the air, and Imus and McCord were working as a well-oiled machine. There was a new producer, Lyndon Abel, and old partners like Larry Kenney to work with. In fact, Larry was just down the hall, playing country music and competing with Don on WYNY, formerly WNBC-FM.

While Imus and McCord seemed to be a winning combination, the choice of Imus's producer may have been more the luck of the draw. Nineteen-year-old Lyndon Abel had to endure the pressure of producing Imus's morning program. With all the bad karma about Imus, he was prepared to turn and run like a rabbit at the first sign of trouble. After hearing Imus do his opening bit as Reverend Hargus that September morning, he not only decided to stay but felt lucky to be working with the best in the business.

The comedy spirit seemed to be alive throughout 30 Rock. Just six flights up from Imus's studio 2 was *Saturday Night Live,* in Studio 8H. "The Not Ready for Prime Time Players" were creating a revolution and the same kind of buzz on Saturday night that Imus would create in the morning.

The next mission for NBC was how to bottle that enthusiasm for Imus that was sending him to the top of the ratings and spread it to the rest of the day. Management would turn to another young disc jockey, this one with roots in New York. His name was Howard Stern.

# 5.
...
# Imus Versus Stern I— The NBC Years

■mus was the king of New York for a few more years. Once ■he returned from Cleveland, he was reborn. He was very proud to say that he had not missed a day his first year back at WNBC. There were great ratings successes, and WNBC was reportedly making a profit. By the summer of 1982 he had turned to other things: cocaine and vodka. Maybe NBC's idea was to do something different with afternoons, or maybe it was just to have a little Imus "insurance" in case 1982 turned into 1973, when Imus missed over a hundred days. Thus, 1982 would be the year the battle would begin. Howard Stern was named afternoon host at 66 WNBC.

You could very well draw a parallel to Imus's rise in the late 1960s and early 1970s to Stern's rise in the late 1970s and early 1980s. While Imus, the rising star of the late 1960s, had cities like Palmdale, Sacramento, and Cleveland on his resumé, Howard Stern, the rising star of the late 1970s, had cities like Hartford, Detroit, and Washington, D.C., on his. Also like Imus, Stern projected New York as the dream job, and who could blame him? He was headed to the top station in the biggest market in the country.

There were two major differences between Stern and Imus as they started off, both of which were probably a factor in how they were perceived and how they handled the arena in which they found themselves. The first factor was age and life experience. In 1971, Imus was thirty-one years old. That made him young, to be sure, but with a lifetime filled with experience in the real world behind him. By then, Imus had lived through his tenure with the marines, was once homeless, and had worked as a uranium miner and railroad worker in addition to the other radio jobs. Stern was four years younger when he arrived on the second floor at 30 Rock, just twenty-eight, his life experiences limited mostly to college and other radio stations. Don knew what other people were going through and how they conducted their lives. Stern's father was even in radio, so Howard was still lacking real-world experience. Only others from Stern's cast, like former air force lieutenant Robin Quivers, knew what things were like in the real world of blue-collar workers.

The second difference may be even more obvious. Stern had an example, maybe even a legend to follow—that of Imus himself. Imus's years in New York coincided nicely with Stern's teenage years on Long Island. As much as Stern may deny it, if you wanted to be in radio and you grew up anywhere near New York City, you knew who Imus was and listened to him. While other people may have preceded him, like Wolfman Jack and Robert W. Morgan, Imus made "shock jock" work in the big city. That made it easier for a station like WNBC to take a flyer on Howard Stern. It had had experience with an opinionated deejay.

Howard Stern grew up on Long Island. The son of a radio engineer, he could listen to the great radio of the sixties and seventies that New York City had to offer. And that best meant Top Forty stations like WABC and WNBC booming across the New York, New Jersey, and Connecticut tristate area. While Imus's love and career goals were music-related, Howard knew he would be more comfortable playing records than singing on them.

About a year after Imus joined WNBC in New York, Stern left Long Island for college. He headed about six hours north on Interstate 95 to Massachusetts and Boston University. After graduating in the mid-1970s, Stern would begin his climb back to New York City with work at stations in Newton, Massachusetts; Westchester County, New York; and Hartford, Detroit, and D.C. Not surprisingly for the radio business, Stern earned about as much doing radio in one of his first jobs in West-chester as Imus did ten years earlier at his first job in Palmdale.

Howard was not exactly an early star, either. While in Hartford, his boss let him leave for Detroit rather than give him a raise of twenty-five dollars a week. His time in Detroit was so "successful" that apparently the station had to change formats. WWWE went from rock to country after less than a year of Howard in the morning.

This is not to say that Stern didn't stir up controversy along the way. Probably the biggest scandal that pre–New York Stern caused was in the nation's capital. On January 13, 1982, one of the most devastating airline crashes in American aviation history occurred when an Air Florida jet taking off from Washington's National Airport crashed into Washington's Four-teenth Street Bridge. As a sampling of things to come, Stern called Air Florida and inquired what the fare would be from the airport to the Fourteenth Street Bridge.

Reports have said that Stern was eventually fired from WWDC over the incident, though it's unlikely that it was the only reason for his leaving. The Air Florida crash happened in January, and Stern wasn't fired until August, three months before his contract was over and only after he had signed a deal with WNBC.

To understand some of what will happen later, it helps to know the mentality behind bringing Howard Stern to New York. The National Broadcasting Company operated several divisions in the early eighties, each segmented into its own domain. So much so that when the company unveiled its new "peacock" logo in 1985, it indicated the reason for a six-feathered bird: Each would represent a division of the network, such as stations, sports, radio, news, and so forth. NBC was on the hunt for a new logo after an early-eighties debacle. Less than a week after they premiered a stylized "N" as their logo, reports discovered that it was the same as Nebraska Public Television.

As part of its "stations" group, NBC owned radio and tele-vision stations around the country, including New York, Chicago, Los Angeles, and Washington, D.C. It was in D.C. that Stern first came to the attention of the NBC brass. It wasn't because he was an important part of the group and they wanted to move him up, as one might expect. It was because Stern was garnering so much of an audience that he was hurting the ratings of the station there, WWRC. So in an "if you can't beat them, hire them away move," NBC offered Stern a contract. New York seemed to be the place to send Stern for two reasons: It would not upset the current talent mix in Washington, and he could improve the flagship's afternoon ratings.

It was another division of NBC, though, that created the first of the problems that would plague the NBC/Stern relationship. In the news division, NBC was trying to promote yet another newsmagazine (though it would be years before they would find the successful formula in *Dateline NBC*). During the most recent incarnation, a Washington-based reporter named Douglas Kiker did a story on the terrible filth that deejays were broadcasting into people's homes every day. His main target was Stern's fart jokes. Kiker declared that the network had actually seen fit to give Mr. Stern a job. As much indigestion as it gave the network brass, though, a contract was a contract. The reality was that Stern had one and WNBC needed the help.

Just after Labor Day, 1982, the Howard Stern show premiered on 66 WNBC, running in the 4 to 8 P.M. time period. According to Stern's accounts, within minutes of arriving in the building, the feud with Imus was on. Stern's movie *Private Parts* portrays the first meeting of the shock jocks. Stern, standing outside Imus's office, was introduced to the I-Man and was verbally abused.

Howard was compared to Imus from the start. He was also pushed to be "more like Imus." All accounts of the period point to WNBC program director Kevin Metheny as the man given the responsibility to make Stern conform, which may have given Stern and Imus the one and only thing in common: lack of respect for Metheny. On the air, Mr. Imus would call him "Kevin Metheny, the Programming Weenie." In Howard's terms, he was "Pig Virus."

It's well documented that Stern was frustrated by restrictions placed on him, especially in the beginning. Even Imus concedes the point that Stern was hired by NBC and then not

# IMUS VERSUS STERN SCORECARD

|  | John Donald Imus | Howard Stern |
|---|---|---|
| Years in radio before arrival at WNBC | 3.5 (June 1968– December 1971) | 6 (1976– September 1982) |
| Years in radio before first book | 14 (*God's Other Son*, July 1981) | 12 (*Private Parts*, October 1993) |
| First movie appearance | *Odd Jobs*, 1985 | *Private Parts*, 1997 |
| First national radio show | New Year's Eve, 1973 | Philadelphia, 1986 |
| First syndication | July 1993 | Philadelphia, August 1986 |
| First television program | *Imus Plus* (WNEW) | *The Howard Stern Show* (WWOR) |
| Number of stations (mid-1998) | approx. 100 | approx. 50 |
| New Jersey location named after them | Children's Hospital | New Jersey Turnpike rest area |

allowed to do the show he was doing. One example of how Howard felt a double standard was applied centered around a "bit" Howard did and how he compared it to those of Imus. One afternoon during Howard's show, his character "God," who usually did the weather, contrived a fake commercial called "Virgin Mary Kong," a takeoff on the popular video game *Donkey Kong,* which had men in a singles bar trying to catch and impregnate the Holy Mother.

Stern was called on the carpet for it, but he had what he must have thought were two good arguments on his side. First was the fact that he had picked on a Christian icon. Stern felt no one would have said a word if he had made it "Buddha Kong" or picked a different religion. This he thought was clearly a double standard. He pointed to Imus's evangelical character, the Right Reverend Dr. Billy Sol Hargus.

What cannot be explained is how Stern could not see the two basic issues that were most obvious to an outside observer. Most of Stern's sketches were more cutting edge, more direct. Imus's style was to attack religion by telling the story through a playful character, something he was taught by the guiding hand of a general manager in Sacramento. Stern's plans called for a no-sacred-cows approach, like weather from God or *Hill Street Jews.* This obviously did not sit well with the NBC brass.

The other issue seems even more basic. By 1982, Imus had been on the air, off and on, for eleven years in New York. He received what can almost be described as a "mandate of the people" in 1979 when he was brought back from Cleveland. Imus knew his job, and he knew New York. He had earned the right to have a twenty-four-hour limo paid for by the station and other perks that went along with being the number-one disc jockey on the number-one station in the number-one city in America. After years of consistent work, he had also earned the right to make his own calls on comedy.

Stern, on the other hand, was still growing. He had had a lot of success at DC101 in the nation's capital, but now he was in New York City. He may have grown up in New York and may have won his spurs in Washington, but he would have to prove himself worthy in the halls of the National Broadcasting Company's headquarters. The flap over "Virgin Mary Kong" was a battle he would not win. Howard was suspended over the segment. While Stern was shocked, NBC was well within its rights. According to the book *Private Parts,* WNBC general manager Dom Fioravanti sent a letter to Stern before he even arrived at the station. In it, rules had been laid out, including no scatological humor and no references to religion.

It was the addition of a new general manager that really started to bring the two men together. About nine months after the start of Stern on WNBC, the administration of Dominic Fioravanti gave way to Randall Bongarten. Even Kevin Metheny was gone. Whether it was intended or not, Bongarten's name would become almost as well known to listeners of WNBC as the names of the morning and afternoon hosts.

Bongarten, like every other general manager who walked through the doors of a broadcasting outlet, made some on-air changes. First of all, Stern received an upgraded time period. Being on from 4 to 8 P.M. caused the end of his show to get cut off by live sports broadcasts that NBC carried, like the New York Knicks and Rangers games. It was not nearly as much of a problem from 3 to 7 P.M., Stern's new time period.

He also decided that the talents of Imus and Stern were what WNBC represented most to listeners and what the station should be built on. The two were paired in a promotion entitled "If we weren't so bad, we wouldn't be so good." It started with a television commercial. Imus and Stern were the stars of WNBC and the talk of New York. The ad capitalized on the bad-boy image of the duo.

The commercial concept was executed very well. The set looked like a TV-anchor desk, with a big 66 WNBC Radio sign hanging on the back wall. On the left sat Imus; on the right, Stern; and in the middle was Randy Bongarten. Bongarten's message was simple: He had drawn the dubious honor of apologizing for his two bad boys. He launched into a list of groups to apologize to, like the National Organization of Women (NOW) and the Jewish Defense League (JDL), glaring at one deejay and then the other where they sat. Stern had a hangdog look on his face. Imus yawned, even snickering at some of the names, and eventually ripped the list from Bongarten's hands and tore it in half. The tag line brought it all together, with a simple Imus voice-over: "Sixty-six WNBC—if we weren't so bad, we wouldn't be so good." A billboard featuring Imus and Stern brought the theme together. Similar ads followed, including one in which "loyal" viewers defaced the billboard.

Imus has been accused of demanding star treatment for the shoot and even walking out, which is probably true. It reportedly took over two hours to get Imus to concede to the shoot and then over thirty takes to get it right. It must have been worth it, though, at least for Bongarten. Now WNBC was no longer just brand Imus; it was Imus and Stern.

While it's obvious the pair both made a living out of making people laugh, it's not well known that they actually shared resources. Though Stern appeared to have a chip on his shoulder about constantly being compared to Imus, Don seemed to like what he saw in Stern. For a while, the relationship was similar to the earlier dealings Imus had with Robert W. Morgan. Imus would drop in on Stern's show on occasion and contribute to the humor. Stern was always willing to put a slap or two in at Imus for good measure. They also shared an eye for good talent.

In the early eighties a Wall Street stockbroker named Al Rosenberg began calling in to the *Imus in the Morning* program and getting on the air on a regular basis. He developed a bit, calling himself Earl C. Watkins. Earl C. Watkins claimed to be the "number-one *Imus in the Mornin'* Fan" and would talk to Imus about his business specials. Earl C. raised Naugas in Naugatuck, Connecticut. Of course, everyone knows that from naugas you get Naugahyde. That was in addition to great products like the coin-operated pacemaker. With the addition of Howard Stern to the WNBC lineup, Rosenberg had a second outlet for his humor.

Before long, Rosenberg quit his job on Wall Street and went to work full-time in radio, commuting from New Jersey to be a voice actor. He would work mornings with Imus, including recording taped pieces for the next day after the show, switch over to Stern's camp, work through the show there, and then sleep in the disc-jockey lounge. Then he started all over the next morning with the I-Man. It may not have measured up to a Wall Street salary, but he was having fun. By the time it was over, Rosenberg ended up working full-time for Stern, and Imus would bring in a promising stand-up named Rob Bartlett.

The year 1984 may not have been the best time in history to be on the radio. One night in June, controversial Denver talk-show host Alan Berg was shot to death. In the wake of the shooting, the *New York Times* talked to some of the big radio talkers of the time. They dug up Larry King, who was on hundreds of radio stations at the time, and old Imus boss Jack Thayer for comments on the tragedy. Of course, they included Imus and Stern. Surprisingly, they were the only two New York radio personalities the *Times* mentioned on the matter. Imus deflected the idea that it could happen to him and went on to trash Berg, saying that he must not have been that good, anyway, if he was on in Denver.

According to the *Times* article, "... one of Mr. Imus's broadcast partners, Howard Stern, is considered a talking tinder box, so ready to cause social combustion—he regularly ridicules homosexuals and various ethnic groups—that WNBC reportedly asked him not to speak to the press at all after Mr. Berg's murder."

It was fun listening to the both of them. Wake up with Imus and drive home with Stern. It was a ritual for many in the tristate area, and their ratings soared. Both ended up number one in their time periods, making WNBC, as Imus would say, "the number-one station in the nation." The station now had to find something to fit in between its two stars. For a while, NBC programmed music, middays, with "Captain" Frank Reed, and his all-request radio show, playing Top Forty hits. Even Imus and Stern would play a few songs, but with FM radio growing stronger and stronger, Top Forty music became less and less important. So NBC relegated music to late night and weekends on the *Time Machine* and brought in a new man to try to bridge the gap between Imus and Stern. Welcome to WNBC, Soupy Sales.

Actually, the addition of Soupy would be preceded by another change. Given his great success at WNBC, Randy Bongarten was moved up the corporate ladder—not surprisingly, since the station was most visible to the corporate execs who worked in the same building. Bongarten had not only brought about ratings success; he had seemingly tamed Imus and Stern—no small feat. So Bongarten was named president of NBC Radio, responsible for all the network-owned-and-operated radio stations and the NBC Radio Network.

Bongarten selected his replacement, and on October 1, 1984, buried in the business section of the *New York Times,* was a two-line announcement that John P. Hayes had been named general manager of WNBC-AM. Seemingly, this announcement signaled the beginning of the end for Stern, for his war with management would soon be heating up again.

Soupy Sales has lived his own life of controversy. A talented comedian, he made a living doing game shows and for a while had several now-classic children's shows. He had even been yanked off the air when he told kids to go into their parents' wallets, take all the little green pieces of paper from their wallets, and mail them to Soupy Sales. It was Hayes, the middleman between Imus and Stern, who solicited Soupy for the position.

Soupy would work from 10 A.M. to 3 P.M., bridging the gap between the two bad boys. He was treated like a star from the start. A piano was brought into the studio for Soupy's accompanist. Lunch would be catered. Soupy would come in early and schmooze with Imus before his show.

The problem was Howard Stern. Stern had spent almost two years trying to gain respect and had finally gotten some of the perks. Now a town car was provided so that he could be driven to and from work, almost a necessity after having become so recognizable. Extra staff had been added to the show. It angered Howard that perks were being handed to Soupy so quickly. The little things even bothered Stern, like coming into a messy studio or the fact that Soupy didn't schmooze with him, as he did with Imus.

Stern was beginning to become his own worst enemy, too.

Even before Soupy, Stern was on the bad side of John P. Hayes. Stern and Randy Bongarten seemed to have a good relationship from the start. In Bongarten's first days, the brash Stern called him on the air and told him not to mess with his show. It was a warning Bongarten took with good humor. When he tried the same trick with Hayes, the boss took it personally. Another popular trick of Stern's was calling Bongarten's wife at home and asking her to give her husband a little extra attention. This was a stunt Hayes would not tolerate.

Of course, managerial changes rarely seemed to affect Imus. His style of "I'm going to do what I want" seemed to remain a constant. He took no guff from management and didn't really need to; his program was number one.

What brought it all to a head seems to be "Bestiality Dial-a-Date." In late September 1985, Stern featured "a lover of animals." The last nail in the coffin came from upper management. Stern's brand of humor did not have a place on the flagship radio station of the National Broadcasting Company. NBC management fired Stern on September 30, 1985.

There is a place for everything. For Stern it was not under the watchful eyes of RCA and NBC executives in the very halls of corporate headquarters. The venue would need to change. Starched shirts were not what Stern was all about; he fit in better with rock and roll. It wouldn't take long for him to find that place.

Once Stern left, his declared goal was to be number one in New York again. He wanted revenge for the poor treatment, perceived or real, that he suffered at the hands of Imus. He signed with a group called Infinity Broadcasting and went to work for Mel Karmazin, a former radio salesman in New York who was building a New York rock station, WXRK. Though Stern started in the afternoons, within six months of leaving WNBC, he would be competing with *Imus in the Morning.*

Imus was hardly up to the challenge. Outside projects had distracted him, and his excessive drinking was taking its toll. It would not be long before Stern would usurp the crown of king of New York. Imus did manage to keep his name in the paper while Stern was getting some press, though.

Imus actually made strides in his role of philanthropist,

though his original intention was less than honorable. In late September 1985, the U.S.S.R. shot down a fully loaded passenger plane on its way to Korea. KAL 007 was shot down for allegedly straying over Soviet airspace, though the Russians would claim no responsibility or culpability.

Imus got his revenge. Thirty Rockefeller Plaza, the RCA Building he worked in, was just a part of the Rockefeller Center complex that included Radio City Music Hall and the famous ice-skating rink. Ringing the skating rink are the flags of all nations. Until Imus got there.

One morning after the tragedy, Imus cut down the Soviet flag from its pole in the plaza. He didn't burn it or desecrate it, as might have been his initial impulse. Instead, Don sold chances to autograph it. The $400,000 in profits all went to the relief fund of the families that lost loved ones in the tragedy.

# 6
# IMUS BRANCHES OUT

Imus had learned early that he could make money in areas other than radio. In fact, one of his first deals was for a record based on his show. In 1972, RCA released *1,200 Hamburgers to Go*. The album, featuring a Jack Davis caricature of Imus sitting in a pile of hamburgers, gave the first real glimpse of the early comedy of Imus to people outside New York, Cleveland, and Sacramento.

The phone prank Imus would continue to be known for more than twenty-five years later leads off the LP: Imus, as Sergeant Kirkland of the Air National Guard, ordering some boxed lunches. Other cuts on the album featured Reverend Hargus.

The success of *1,200 Hamburgers to Go* led to a second album in 1973, entitled *One Sacred Chicken to Go* (RCA). Jack Davis again did the cover art. The Right Reverend Dr. Billy Sol was back, too. The "A" side of the album is much like a miniature Billy Sol Hargus radio show. You can almost imagine yourself back when, with your hand on the radio one Sunday night, listening to the reverend preach and sing! Billy Sol Hargus singing is just part of the first side of the album, rocking to the gospel tune "Hey Billy Sol, Won't You Please Heal Us All." You can also find out about flying to heaven on Hebrew National or picking up some chicken that's so holy, "it won't soil your dishes." All available from Dr. Hargus's First Church of the Gooey Death and Discount House of Worship for "a limited time, and a limited time only."

Imus's third album would break the mold of the first two. Instead of using bits he played on the radio, he brought his stand-up act to the record-buying public. The album cover to *This Honkey's Nuts* (1974 Bang Records) featured a photo of Imus instead of a Jack Davis illustration. On the front cover Don was posed wearing his cowboy hat, his tongue sticking out, hair down around his shoulders, and wearing a denim jacket. The back featured several smaller photos and a large one of a crazed-looking Imus, looking almost demon-eyed, in full attack mode. It also featured a prominent warning that would make Tipper Gore proud—that the album was X-rated.

It was, too. Just a glance at the first track will tell you that: "Swear With Flair." It's barely several seconds into the album before Imus launches into this bit, complete with all of George Carlin's "Top Seven" and many more colorful and interesting choices. The "B" side features "Reverend Billy Sol Hargus Confesses" along with "Imus in Washington," coauthored by Charles McCord. McCord actually gets coauthor credit on all of the bits written by Imus except the Reverend Billy riff, showing that the collaboration of McCord and Imus was alive and well even in the early seventies.

Imus released several singles as well. The early ones, in the fifties and sixties, were on labels like Challenge, RV, and Delphi. In 1971, Imus launched a comedy record upon an unsuspecting nation. The 45 bore the title "The Ballad of Rick (Don't Call Me Ricky 'Cause I Am a Veteran) Nelson." The flip side of this vinyl treasure is "From Adam's Rib to Women's Lib." The people responsible? Happy Tiger Records in Los Angeles. RCA, the parent company of NBC, was responsible for another Imus 45. "Son of Checkers" attacked President Nixon's famous Checkers speech in a 1973 record.

If you are collecting Imus memorabilia, the records usually run between fifteen and sixty dollars apiece. The most collectible piece of Imus stuff is the bobble-head doll, a little ceramic doll with an oversized Imus head on it, given out right after Imus moved to WFAN. President Clinton had one on his private desk for a while. Finding one is difficult. Fans seem to be hoarding them, and the two I have come across have both sold for over one hundred dollars—a very good investment for the seller, especially when the I-Man gave them away on the air free.

In 1981, not quite two years after returning to NBC, Imus was putting the finishing touches on his first book, his only novel to date. *God's Other Son* chronicled the life of probably his most famous character, the Right Reverend Dr. Billy Sol Hargus.

By far, Reverend Hargus has been Imus's most successful character. The evangelist character was so popular that when Imus hosted 1972's *Billboard* Awards, he did the entire show as Hargus, the first character Imus utilized when he returned to WNBC as "God's Chosen, Re-Rosen Disc Jockey" in 1979.

When reading *God's Other Son*, anyone who has listened to Imus for more than a few days will pick up what seems to be quite a few references to his life. A lot may be subtle, just little throwaways, but they can be found. Of course, they will also pick up the not-so-subtle sexual references that make this Imus book strictly for adults only.

Under the classification "Cameo Appearances" you will find Imus's longtime engineer at WNBC, who makes it into the book as a birth announcement: "Harry Tucker and wife had a boy." Charles McCord didn't make it, but his alter ego, Frank McCord, is the reverend's private pilot. Interestingly enough, McCord at one time had a private pilot's license.

Familiar Imus locations are also used to tell the story. Billy Sol's biggest day happens, of course, in New York. Palmdale, California, is the location of a psychic in the book, and Hargus's media consultant freaked out, saying that if he got into trouble in New York he'd be banished to, of all places, Cleveland.

Careful reading of the dedication will tell you a few things about Imus's life and who his friends are. The 1981 version of *God's Other Son* has two pages of name-dropping thank-yous that show off a couple of Imus's favorite media friends. Jeffrey Katzenberg, then of Paramount and now of Dreamworks, is mentioned; Imus threatens him for a movie deal. The book is dedicated to Michael Lynne, Imus's longtime lawyer. Even the enigmatic Harriet Imus receives a thank-you in this version.

In the 1994 reissue, while the content of the book stays the same, the front and end notes are changed. Imus trashes Simon & Schuster for publishing the novel just to take advantage of his now-national reach. In the acknowledgments, Imus picks on Michael Lynne once more and again threatens that there'd better be a movie deal, this time with Lynne's New Line Cinema. No Harriet mention this time, though. Now he thanks deirdre Coleman (yes, lower-case *d* for some reason) for being his significant other.

Two general side notes about the book: While a movie never came about, supposedly there is a script, *God's Other Son: The Musical,* with songs by Kinky Friedman. Also, note the name change on the reverend. In the early years, it's Hargis with an I; later, it changes to Hargus.

The fast rise and hard fall of both Imus and Hargus beg comparison. The original *God's Other Son* appeared in 1981, just two years after Imus returned from Cleveland, where he had gone after falling from grace in New York. It's difficult to think that Imus wasn't believing his own press. He rocketed so fast to the top, garnering two major awards, and had the job of a lifetime in 1971; after just four years in the business, he probably felt justified in calling himself "God's Chosen Disc Jockey." It's as obvious now as it probably was then that it was tough billing to live up to. Imus had been due for a fall.

*God's Other Son* was a bestseller. The cover of the 1981 edition features an illustration of a preacher, light beaming down on him as he walks on water. The 1994 reissue is Bible-black. It was in 1987, though, that the book would probably have the most impact on Don's life.

Then there was Imus in the movies. In 1984 a gang of stand-up comedians, including Jake Steinfeld, Paul Reiser, and Robert Townsend, joined together to make the movie *Odd Jobs.* The HBO Pictures production centers around the summer jobs of four college students and their various encounters. One of them decides to sell vacuum cleaners and comes across the character of Monty Leader.

Monty Leader is Don Imus. If you are thinking of rushing out and picking up this epic, you may want to think again. He's in the movie for about eighteen seconds. In short, the movie stinks.

The brief appearance wasn't exactly beyond Imus's range. The best way to describe it would be "God's Other Vacuum

Cleaner Dealer." Dressed in a pink tuxedo with ruffled shirt, Imus preaches at his salespeople to sell these nuclear-powered house suckers. Yes, it was "Monty's Vacuum Cleaner Co. God's favorite vacuum! Suck it up for Jesus!" If there had been a real Right Reverend Dr. Billy Sol Hargus, Imus would have made him proud.

In the early 1980s, a new phenomenon was taking over the music industry. Just as FM radio lured us away from listening to static-filled songs on AM and reenergized music, MTV was leading the way in a whole new area of the music industry. The format for MTV was very similar to radio at the time: Play some music clips and have some disc jockeys, now called video jockeys, chat in between the videos.

While MTV was attracting viewers in their teens and early twenties, older audiences, those who preferred Kenny Rogers to Duran Duran, were left unserved. So the people at Viacom, who owned MTV, decided to spin off a new channel, which would appeal to older audiences. To launch the network, they hired a man who had shot his way up the radio ladder, making waves before and after he landed at WNBC in New York. They hired Bob Pittman.

Pittman's job was to develop the network called Video Hits One or VH-1. With the success of MTV as a guide, the format seemed perfectly appropriate. Pittman set out to hire video jockeys.

With much fanfare in late 1984, the same man who fired Imus in 1977 and rehired him in 1979 picked John Donald Imus to be the first VH-1 veejay. Articles in music trade magazines like *Billboard* and *Variety* announced the selection. Don Imus would lead the group and receive a fairly free hand to bring his act to television. Since Pittman and director of programming Kevin Metheny were both WNBC management alumni, they knew what they were getting with Imus.

Three other people joined the clip-introducing crew. Two other New York disc jockeys were selected to be premier VH-1 veejays. Brash Scott Shannon, from New York's Z-100, the original "morning zookeeper," got one of the nods. So did the soulful Frankie Crocker, who was tops at New York's urban station WBLS. The first four were rounded out by a musician-entertainer named Jon Bauman, who gained fame as Bowser in the act Sha Na Na. This "Fab Four" would lead off the network starting New Year's Day, 1985. Of the four, Imus was the premier veejay, so he led off the launching of VH-1. Singer Rita Coolidge joined the veejay ranks before the end of the first year.

The reviews of the project didn't take long to start coming in. *People Weekly* reviewed it twice in the first seven months. *Rolling Stone* weighed in, and even *Newsweek* had an opinion. They were all about the same: The videos were tame, like watching grass grow. The headlines tell it all. *Newsweek:* "Soft Rock and Hard Talk"; *Rolling Stone:* "VH-1 a big snooze"; and, probably most important, *Billboard* in 1986: "MTV Networks Making Major Changes at VH-1." Shannon seemed to hit the nail on the head over the problems. He told *Newsweek:* "Don comes closer to duplicating his radio personality." That seemed to be a major problem, especially where Imus and Shannon were concerned. Their radio jobs were not just about introducing records; they were personality radio. Shannon had to leave his sound effects and sidekicks at the radio studio. Imus couldn't very easily launch into a Crazy Bob bit. Another potential problem: Just what was there for them to do in front of a camera? Radio is theater of the mind. When you hear a crash, you can picture the cars slamming together; the visual medium is a lot more dependent on images. What most people got, though, was Don or Frankie Crocker on a standard veejay set with very little visual appeal. The second video experiment finally ended after a couple of years for Imus. He would go back to radio, for a while, anyway.

In October 1987, Imus would change his life once and for all. He was spending time on a book tour, promoting the reissue of *God's Other Son*. He was alone in a hotel room when he finally hit rock bottom.

# 7
# REACHING BOTTOM

Imus was a drunk. In Alcoholics Anonymous (AA), they would probably say he still is a drunk, but *was* seems the appropriate tense in this case. He was not a "I have one too many martinis at lunch every day" drunk but a "drink out of the bottle; get me some more vodka" drunk. Kinky Friedman once reminded Imus: "You were so high you needed a stepladder to scratch your butt."

His drinking seemed to take hold as his radio career blossomed. He was required to be "on" more now, meeting fans and clients and making appearances. He would drink with his coworkers. Imus told Larry King how he used to drink with Murray the K and Cousin Brucie. A lot of mornings he would come in and talk of places like the Lone Star Café Road House, and T.J. Tuckers.

He was also a drug addict: pills when he could get them, cocaine in massive quantities. He told *Newsweek* in 1985 that his habit was costing him up to four thousand dollars a week at one point. He would even cut his own stuff with various powders, like carpet fresheners. In the seventies, while on the air, Imus told about how great it used to be when the record companies would give him drugs to get their records played. In one clip, you can practically hear him begging, though humorously, for a record-company promotion man to visit and bring some stuff. In the nineties, he would even feign confusion when a record company asked him to play a song and didn't offer him any coke as an incentive.

Imus had claimed to clean up his act numerous times before. When he left Cleveland in 1979, he was described as more focused. When he started at VH-1, he said he had turned his life around. He claims that he finally kicked the coke habit in the summer of 1983. He was still drinking, even going drunk to AA meetings. Though he claimed sobriety, he would leave the meetings and pick up a bottle on the way home. One thing that surprised him was the people in AA. He expected winos but met corporate executives instead.

In 1987 he finally hit the skids. It's hard to know if any one thing triggered the need to get help. His morning show had been sliding in the ratings, first from an attack by Scott Shannon and the *Z Morning Zoo* and then by former WNBC afternoon guy Howard Stern. Imus's decline could have been the result of Stern's growth in popularity in the mornings and the stiffer competition or the stress of work and all those mornings getting up at 4 A.M. Perhaps he just could not put the vodka bottle to his lips or the coke up his nose one more time.

Most of his drinking took place while he was working at WNBC. It's central to a lot of stories about Imus the Drunk. He told this story in the spring of 1998. From listening to it, one would guess it took place in the early seventies, but Imus didn't give the date. It seems one day the I-man had a monster drunk going. When it was time to head home, he headed across the street to fetch his car. He sat down on a bench in the Rockefeller Center parking garage and proceeded to fall dead asleep (though pass out might be more accurate). He awoke, still dressed in his Indian jewelry and belt, and discovered it was morning. He wandered across the street and went back to work.

Then there is the story that Bernie loves to give him hell about. It seems that one time while working at 30 Rock, Don needed to relieve himself. Instead of a restroom, he used the first semiprivate area available to him—a phone booth. Yes, he peed in a phone booth in the corporate headquarters of NBC. One of his record producers claims he once peed in a plate at a fancy restaurant. He was losing control.

The story of Bernard McGuirk's first day had to be a shock to the new producer. He took over for Lyndon Abel in 1983, and what a welcome! It seems that the new Mr. McGuirk, walking down the hall, discovered Mr. Imus, in his underwear, screaming at people at the top of his lungs.

It's not quite the welcome Howard Stern's replacements got. Joey Reynolds and his sidekick, Big Jay Sorensen, had been on the air about a month when the topic turned to Imus. They devoted an afternoon to talking about Don and Fred's records from the sixties as well as a song Joey had cut called "Rats in My Room." Right in the middle of one of Don's songs, the hotline rang. It was the I-Man. Big Jay, who was running the controls, claims that their producer told him to bail out of the song and put Imus on the air.

Imus said, "Hey Joey, I made more money on that record than you made in your whole FUCKING career."

Thank God for delay, right? Wrong. They had dumped out of delay a couple of minutes earlier to do the traffic report, and it had not caught up yet. Therefore, while Sorensen's finger pounded the delay, Imus's comment was already out over the air. Imagine his shock when, after only having been at NBC a month and not being a traditional NABET engineer, "every manager and engineer in the then RCA building came running into the studio . . . while we were still on. I thought my career was over . . . that quickly."

Sorensen got called on the carpet by the program director, and so did Imus. The I-Man had to record an on-air apology that aired frequently the next day and may have even gotten a day off: suspended. Sorensen still had to pass Imus in the halls, though, and he thinks the I-Man may have whispered, "Fuck you," during one of those passes. Sorensen did get a lovely Christmas gift from Imus, however.

The goal of being on radio is to get people to listen. Imus had two classic ways of promoting himself. The single Imus came up with a plan to meet someone—anyone. Usually, the name of the game when you are even the lowest of celebrities is that you don't date groupies. Not only did Imus date them; he held a contest. The "Win a Date With Imus" contest got a young woman a limo ride and dinner with Don. Imus could have taken her to the Rainbow Room or any other fancy New York nightspot; instead he took his winning date to a rest area on the New Jersey Turnpike. Imagine the wonder of dining from a table overlooking the gas pumps.

The other promo came during the dark days of WNBC, when rumors were running rampant about its impending sale. One morning, Imus came on the air and said he and McCord were going to appear on *Live at 5,* WNBC-TV's local newscast, with a "big announcement." The speculation was running rampant. Was Imus the buyer? Would he save the big 66?

The moment finally came, and Imus made his announcement. The $66,000 joke contest was coming to WNBC radio. P. T. Barnum was probably smiling in his grave at the suckers who fell for that one.

Even with all the pressures squarely on him, John Donald Imus Jr. knew that the time had finally come to break his bad habits. With help from his friends, in July 1987, (possibly accompanied by WNBC program director Dale Parsons), he checked himself into the Hanley Hazelden Center in West Palm Beach, Florida, and finally got himself clean and sober. He's still taking it one day at a time—ten years later.

He often says that he was luckier than he should have been. He got too many breaks. Aside from perhaps Mike Lynne and Charles McCord, most people looked the other way instead of offering to help.

One thing that Imus could count on was the support of his friends and his bosses. NBC chairman Bob Wright was one of the first to step up and stand behind Imus. Wright has the reputation as one of the most loyal executives in the business. Years later, he also supported NBC West Coast president Don Ohlmeyer through his rehab, just to name one.

Imus took his rehab seriously. He went through the twelve steps of the program and had some interesting encounters along the way. One of the steps requires that you divulge all your problems, so he sat down with a counselor and started to spill his guts. The reply he received was "That's it?"

His motto was that he was not going to try and bullshit anyone about his problems, and he keeps to it now. When he travels, he has all the liquor taken from the hotel rooms just to remove the temptation.

When he got back to WNBC, things were changing. RCA, the Radio Corporation of America, which had owned NBC since the thirties, turned over the reins to General Electric (GE) in 1986. The FCC, in charge of broadcasting, had seen the need, in the early eighties, to begin to break up the big media groups. This meant that GE could not continue to own multiple stations in one market. WNBC-AM and WYNY-FM would have to be split from WNBC-TV in New York. The same thing would happen in Chicago, San Francisco, Washington, D.C., and so on.

Given the option of selling the radio or the television stations, the choice was obvious. NBC Television was far more profitable than NBC Radio. Plus, while the NBC Television Network was turning around, with an upswing in ratings and profits, thanks to programs like *The Cosby Show,* things were not as good for the radio division. According to information released to potential buyers, the red ink was flowing. While WNBC-AM had very profitable years during the Imus and Stern era, according to information printed in the *New York Times,* the cash flow had dropped steadily since 1983.

Things were not much better for WYNY, though there was promise. Changes in the marketplace enabled WYNY to go country. It seems the station that had been the country outlet for years, WHN, also had changed hands. Now owned by an Indianapolis firm named Emmis Broadcasting, owner Jeff Smulyan dropped the country-music format and started a new radio format, all sports, all the time.

The estimates varied widely on what the stations might be worth, though any buyer would have to be someone with deep pockets, for two reasons. First, no station in the major markets like New York and Chicago would go cheaply; second, the group would have to be able to absorb the red ink. Two groups emerged as the lead runners, according to the *New York Times.* The first was the group from Indianapolis, Emmis Broadcasting. The second was a new group, Quantum Media.

In what can only be perceived as strong irony, the head of Quantum was very familiar to Imus. If Quantum's gambit was successful, Imus would once again be working for Bob Pittman, the former WNBC and MTV executive who headed the new group. That would mark the fourth time the two were brought

## ADJECTIVES USED TO DESCRIBE THE I-MAN

- satirist (*Broadcasting & Cable*)

- curmudgeon (*Advertising Age*)

- liberal (*Time* magazine)

- crude, sophisticated (*Detroit News*)

- a household word in New York (Murray the K)

- a hip granny playing R & B on the church organ (*Time*)

- the thinking man's shock jock (*New York Daily News*)

- morning madman (*Connecticut* magazine)

together. It didn't happen, though. On February 20, 1988, the *Times* reported that NBC had okayed a deal for the sale of six NBC-owned stations to Emmis.

Just a couple of days later, Imus and McCord ranted on the air about the announcement of the sale. While no one knew what was going to happen, Imus and McCord screamed at the salespeople, "It's over!" Imus said that anything would be better than the last four years at NBC: "Soupy Sales, give me a break!" and "The time machine sucks!"

A juggling act followed for Emmis Broadcasting. Smulyan owned too many stations in New York—four to be exact. When the details finally became clear, Emmis kept its current FM station, sold WYNY and its 1050 frequency, and announced that WFAN would move down the dial, soon to be heard on the clear channel 660.

While Imus, McCord, and new producer Bernard McGuirk would make the switch to Astoria, along with a couple of sports guys (most notably Mike Breen and Dave Simms), it wasn't good news for many employees. Some, mostly engineering staff, would be reshuffled in the NBC empire. Many would become unemployed, Big Jay Sorensen among them. Sorensen encountered a most gracious I-Man. "One morning just before the end, in October of 1988, he came into a production room where I was making an audition tape and said that I was one of the best jocks to come through NBC in a while and that I would be fine. He smiled and left. So, Imus is a swell guy."

WYNY was the first to go. On September 23, 1988, the transfer took effect. The FM station was turned over to Westwood One, a large distributor of radio programming nationwide. There was very little fanfare over that change as compared to ones at WNBC.

On October 7 most of WNBC's regular afternoon programming was preempted by a special retrospective, *WNBC, the First 66 Years.* The *Alan Colmes Show* did air, though, with famous voices from the past years on NBC voicing their memories. Alan Colmes would go down in history with the dubious honor of being the last voice heard on WNBC. NBC's flagship station would depart the air, leaving Radio City without radio for the first time. Colmes wrapped it all up by saying, "For the last time, this is WNBC, New York."

PART II

THE
SECOND
COMING
OF IMUS

# 8
...
# SPORTS RADIO

T here was a short pause. Within seconds of the sign-off, the New York radio frequency that had been home to only three different sets of call letters, WEAF, WNBC (twice), and WRCA, would get a fourth set and, more spectacular, only its third owner, the first real new one since the 1930s. Emmis Broadcasting owner, Jeff Smulyan, would be the man who would hopefully make sports radio a success.

After the short pause of WNBC permanently dropping from the airways at 6:15 P.M. on that Friday in October, the voice of Charles McCord announced a station ID. It was immediately followed by the familiar Imus character of the Right Reverend Dr. Billy Sol Hargus. "God's Only Chosen, Re-Rosen Disc Jockey" was now on Sports Radio. The changeover was simulcast on WNBC TV, with Al Roker doing the honors live from the parking lot of the Mets-Dodgers National League Playoff game.

It hadn't been an easy fifteen months to get to that point. July 1, 1987, marked the day that country music died and Emmis brought sports talk to former country station 1050 WHN. The first sports radio station in the country, Sports Radio 1050 WFAN, was on the air, with marquee names like Greg Gumbel, Jim Lampley, and a Cleveland import named Pete Franklin. They broadcast the Mets games live, but they struggled to find a real niche.

The purchase of WNBC's frequency supercharged the young station, however, with benefits in every area. The frequency itself was a gold mine; 660 AM in New York is a 50,000-watt clear-channel station, protected from local stations east of the Rockies at night. So, with even a decent radio, WFAN could now be heard in thirty-eight states.

Another big benefit was the addition of more live sports. Starting off with only baseball kept the station busy in the summer, but "hot-stove league" talk in the winter isn't as popular as actual games. WNBC had long been the home of the live radio broadcasts of New York Knicks basketball and New York Rangers hockey. Now WFAN would have live sports year-round.

WFAN's biggest draw, though, would be the guy whose office moved but time slot and dial position didn't: Don Imus. Now, instead of commuting from his home near Central Park to 30 Rock, Imus would head to the Astoria section of Queens and broadcast from the radio studios buried deep in a basement.

It didn't take long for Imus to settle into a routine in his new studio. No more overlooking the ice-skating rink. Now the only scenery was Big Bird, the *Sesame Street* character whose show was also in the same facility. One thing was familiar, though: the friction between Imus and the afternoon guy. After a hiatus once Stern left and some minor swearing at Joey Reynolds, Imus had a new foe, "Old Acid Breath," Pete Franklin. Franklin was, as his nickname describes, a crusty sports fan who would take calls and then insult callers from three to seven every day. For the most part, Franklin was the star of the station pre-Imus. He held the distinction of being one of the premier "fan-ies," if you will. The other originals, people like Greg Gumbel and Jim Lampley, had quickly gone by the wayside. Much like Imus, Franklin gained acclaim as a king of his particular type of broadcasting, sports-fan talk shows. Recruited from Cleveland's WWWE after almost fifteen years, Franklin was the talk of the New York area. That is, until WFAN took over WNBC.

There was no doubt about who the king of Astoria was now. Franklin got his shots in at WFAN's new star morning man. I am sure it was not a surprise attack to Imus. He certainly had to know of Franklin, since the two had both worked in Cleveland at the same time and word gets around. Plus, this was Pete Franklin's shtick.

The war was on. Imus would get tapes of Franklin's show

and play the best or worst of them, depending on how you look at it the next morning. How old was Pete Franklin? Well, the Imus posse would try to guess in skits. They knew Franklin would be on that afternoon if his name was not in the obituaries that morning.

With all that, it only took about a year before Pete was run off. He still says, from somewhere in San Diego, that playing New York was like "playing the palace." A new crew came on in afternoons, one that Imus had a hand in creating. In the meantime, there were other targets for the special brand of Imus's venom. How about the boss? It worked back in 1971 when Don called his bosses "Mr. Vicious" and "Mr. Numb."

The general manager of WFAN was Scott Meyer, brought to New York from Minneapolis by Emmis Broadcasting. Imus dubbed Meyer "Pizza Face," though as long as Imus was the advertising-billing king of New York, he could call the general manager whatever he wanted. *Crain's New York Business* named Meyer one of "Forty Under Forty." Meyer was immortalized by Rob Bartlett with a song parody, too. Rob rocked with "We Didn't Like Scott Meyer" to the tune of Billy Joel's "We Didn't Start the Fire." Gumby was the program director at the "Fan." Not the big green clay being but Mark "Gumby" Mason.

With the move to Sports Radio, one can guess that sports became a more important part of the show. Imus needed a sportscaster. For a while it was "the great Don Criqui." Criqui was doing play-by-play for NBC Sports (he's now with the NFL on CBS) but would come in and do sports for the show. Criqui still calls in from time to time and usually tells terrible old jokes with a very dry delivery.

With Criqui on the road, especially for football and basketball games, a sub kept busy warming up in the bullpen. Imus, who has an eye for good talent, picked a guy who really caught his eye. Chris Russo was an up-and-coming sports talk-show host and had made his way from Florida to weekends on New York's WMCA radio. "Mad Dog" Russo got the nod to be the fill-in as *Imus in the Morning* sports guy.

Russo paired up with a behind-the-scenes guy from CBS Sports. Virtually a no-name with the public, inside broadcasting sports circles said he was a guru. His specialty was football and college basketball, and he had spent a few months working weekends at the Fan. Mike Francessa would attract the attention of the I-Man as well. In one guest appearance on the morning show, Francessa and Imus were discussing the NCAA Basketball Tournament. Mike went out on a limb and predicted that Seton Hall University's Pirates would make the final four. Imus, in total disbelief, said he would buy Francessa a Porsche if they did. Not only did the Seton Hall Pirates make the final four; they made the finals. Did Francessa get the Porsche? Well . . . Seton Hall's loss took Mike's Porsche with it. Sometime later, Imus handed Francessa a toy Porsche as a consolation prize.

Imus did have to pay off one bet, though. After jumping on the Seton Hall bandwagon, the I-Man predicted that there was no way the Fordham Rams would beat the Pirates. Fordham won, and Imus had to wash the team's jockstraps. He did deliver them, though, and spent the game sitting on the bench with the team. After a quick start, the Rams lost by over twenty.

The popularity of Mike and the Mad Dog individually on weekends and on the Imus program gave the bosses at WFAN the courage to put the pair together as a replacement for Pete Franklin. *Mike and the Mad Dog* premiered in the afternoon slot in September 1989. The promotion for WFAN now featured Imus, Russo, and Francessa in caricature form, holding footballs, baseballs, and basketballs. The tag line—"We've got New York Sports by the . . ."

Once the pair were together, it would be Imus's continuing mission to split them up. He would walk by them in the hall and say, "You are so much better than [the other guy]." He did play peacemaker during several of the more public fights, however.

Imus's friends have always been a big part of the show, even if they are small in stature. That would be mostly true for Mike Lupica. Lupica is a New York sportswriter who dabbles in broadcasting, mostly by being a frequent contributor on Imus's show, *Good Morning America,* and ESPN's *Sports Reporters.* Lupica has been one of Imus's best friends off and on for years.

If Imus had had a small hand in creating trouble for Mike and the Mad Dog, he created a great deal of trouble for Lupica. WFAN was making a move to replace their sagging midday program. At the same time Imus joined the station, Bill Mazer joined the middays, live from Mickey Mantle's restaurant in Manhattan. (Imus's favorite line: "Look for Mickey under the table.") Mazer's show consisted of chatting with sports celebrities over lunch. (Once, not long after his show premiered, he had supermodel Kathy Ireland in the guest seat. Mazer got a reply he didn't expect to an innocent question. He asked Kathy if her husband was a doctor, and she replied, "Yeah, he's a proctologist, so he spends all day looking at assholes.")

So WFAN planned a new team; the outspoken Mike Lupica would be joined by Len Berman. (Berman is the WNBC-TV sportscaster who appears on NBC's *Today* show with his "Spanning the World" segment of sports bloopers every month.) Actually, the original team should have been Lupica and WWOR sportscaster Russ Salzberg, but Salzberg had a conflict with his other job. So Berman signed on the dotted line and, according to the *New York Daily News*, before the show even started, tried to renegotiate his contract.

Imus didn't really help bring the parties together, either. Being strongly in the Lupica camp, Imus attacked Berman as "Lenny the Jew" and joked that Berman was just his lunch boy. Imus also joked about Lupica, who had long been one of his best friends, a distinction that gets one no advantage whatsoever. On March 31, 1993, by a twist of fate, the pair premiered together, and Berman, in his first broadcast retaliation, attacked Imus, while Lupica sat it out. On April 1, probably a lucky April Fool's Day for Lupica, Berman and Lupica each had their own two-hour chunk of time. After one day there was no chance of pairing them up. Berman lasted four months, and Lupica lasted until October 1993, when Imus had a whole new set of midday hosts to torture, the previously mentioned Russ Salzberg, along with Steve Somers, a WFAN vet.

While the sports games inside the station were interesting, the outside world of sports did not go unnoticed. It was during the NBA's 1993 playoffs that Imus got to revel in the agony of another; this time it was Malik Sealy. Sealy, who played for the Indiana Pacers at the time, had lost his playbook at Kennedy Airport. Where did it end up? In that basement in Astoria, on the *Imus in the Morning* program. So, with the Pacers getting ready to take on the Knicks, Imus began to recite the playbook on the air. Hey, you gotta help the home team.

Even a desperate call by Sealy to Imus didn't stop the morning mouth. The Knicks won the first two games of the series. Was the playbook a factor? We'll never know for sure.

Imus loves to watch sports. Of course, working at a station that goes by the name Sports Radio helps fuel anyone's sports interest, but the I-Man is a sports fan. You could easily say his teams are whoever is winning at the time, after all, that means someone must be losing and is thus due for a hammering. In reality, though, he has his favorites. The Los Angeles Dodgers would probably head up his baseball list, since he lived in Los Angeles and Southern California in his late teens and early twenties. Imus did show up at Shea Stadium one opening day to cheer on the Mets from the television booth. A great move, because with a record of 0-0, Imus was not getting behind a losing team. He will probably admit to spending most of his time these days watching the New York teams, since they show up on television most often. He recently said his favorite sports are wrestling, car racing, and football, so who really knows but him?

One can get him out to play once in a great while, too. That is, if one asks nicely and appeals to his charitable side. Imus does have a big heart.

Actress Susan St. James, a wonderful woman who is totally dedicated to the cause of the Special Olympics, teamed up with Taylor Lupica (Mike Lupica's wife) to raise funds for St. James's favorite charity. In August 1991 they hosted a celebrity softball and tennis tournament to benefit the Connecticut Special Olympics. Ms. St. James worked on the NBC side, drafting her husband, Dick Ebersol, president of NBC Sports, to help. Ms. Lupica went to work on her husband's friends and associates at WFAN.

Rob Bartlett, Mike and the Mad Dog, and Imus all pitched in to help. So did a lot of celebrities: Bob Costas, Pat Riley, TV star Larry Drake, and a host of others joined in the fun. Leading off the day at Yale University was a softball game. Bartlett joined with the World Wrestling Federation's Vince McMahon on the play-by-play, while Macho Man Randy Savage called balls and strikes. Imus dropped by and was inserted into the lineup. The I-Man grounded into a double play and, in a moment caught on camera, tripped over first base. Imus shouldn't feel too bad, though. He joined Bartlett and McMahon in the booth just in time to watch Governor Weicker hit into a double play as well.

Imus was only a walk-on in the softball game; he was actually scheduled for celebrity tennis. He umpired, played, and commented as well. What team won? Who cares? Since fans packed the stadium for both events, the children and adults of the Special Olympics were ultimately the winners.

Speaking of tennis, Imus loves it. Not that he plays a lot; running seems to be the only sport he actually participates in, but he loves to talk tennis. For years you could see him in the stands out in Flushing Meadows, at the U.S. Open, held in late August and early September in New York. Imus had his own reserved seats for almost twenty years and spent time with cronies Donald Trump, Mike Wallace, and Pat O'Brien.

He frequently comments on tennis players during his radio show, though he seems to favor talking about women tennis stars. For example, he might imagine just about any female tennis player in a pile in Martina Navratilova's hotel room. Or he might be hoping for a hot, humid, sweaty day on which the white tennis outfits take on a see-through quality.

Bud Collins is Imus's resident tennis pro. Collins appears several times during the majors each year to comment on tennis's goings-on. Well, maybe not during the Australian Open; the line has to be drawn somewhere. Imus can usually suck him in to saying something hideous, too, which is why Collins ranks right up there as one of Don's better guests.

New York is not just the home of the U.S. Open, though. As much as it plays host to larger-than-life events and teams, it is a home for even larger egos. Three of the biggest belong Don Imus, Donald Trump, and George Steinbrenner, and when they clash, it's nothing short of spectacular. The two have been Don's friends off and on, but as of this writing, they're off.

Trump, the millionaire businessman, has at times been one of Imus's biggest defenders, and the reverse is true, too. Imus used to defend the generally unpopular Trump.

The feud may have sparked like a powder keg in 1992. Imus felt the need to trash "the Donald's" Atlantic City properties, since two of them had to declare bankruptcy in order to reorganize their debt. Trump defended his properties by pulling his advertising dollars from the station. Imus accused Trump of being a deadbeat; Trump claimed Imus was funnier when he was drinking. That didn't stop Imus from broadcasting from one of Trump's hotels before a Holyfield-Foreman fight and harassing Trump for good measure.

One of the more recent and more public clashes occurred on the pages of the *New York Post* in early 1998. The I-Man lashed out at Trump for being a "Howard Stern butt boy" and attacked the sales of Trump's latest book. The Donald swung back at Imus by attacking his ratings. What a couple of millionaire boys won't do to get attention.

Imus has not gone easy on Big Stein, either. When the Yankees' owner began his annual whining about needing a new stadium, Imus did some investigating. First, he sent Bernard to the Bronx to check on Steinbrenner's assertion that it was unsafe. Bernie spent the morning talking to the "natives" and handing out little brown bags with cans of beer in them. "Barron von Steingrabber" (as Mike Lupica would call him) is actually a big Imus fan and booked himself on the show one day to talk about it.

While one might think at this point it got ugly, it was just the opposite. Imus and Steinbrenner joked and had a terrific time needling each other. When Imus wanted to know why Steinbrenner wanted the Yankees moved from the Bronx, Steinbrenner asked him when he had last been to a Yankee game. Imus pointed out it had been twenty years. When all was said and done, though, Imus had gotten Steinbrenner to admit that if a new stadium was built for the Yankees, he would pay for part of it. Imus was again breaking news in the tabloids. We like it when our millionaires get along.

A locker room may have been a great comparison for not only the FAN's location but the Imus program in general. You couldn't miss a couple of women who were playing a big role in the game that was the Imus show. The "voices" of Diane Sawyer, Leona Helmsley, and other female characters were brought to life by Jane Gennaro on tape. Live during the show, Imus had Eileen Marchese, the traffic reporter, to abuse.

Abuse he did. Marchese, who most of the time delivered her reports from the remote location of the World Trade Center, took a verbal bashing. Imus would ask her if she had had sex the night before, when her wedding to Steve Cohen (the board operator for Mike and the Mad Dog) would take place, and whether she was wearing pants. She spent seven or eight years on the Imus show, outlasting Gennaro.

Gennaro, the female equivalent of Rob Bartlett and Larry Kenney, lasted only a few years in the boys' locker room of the Imus program. She did have some memorable characters while she patrolled the hallways of Astoria, though, dropping by for weekly taping sessions. Aside from the previously mentioned Diane Sawyer, Gennaro did people like hotel queen Leona Helmsley and Joan Rivers as well. Gennaro characterizes her time working on the Imus program as being the "one sister to six brothers." She actually was a traffic reporter herself, breaking in at WNBC. She eventually would leave the Imus show to continue her one-woman shows on Broadway.

Politics caught Imus's interest long before the Persian Gulf caught his eye in 1990. After all, this was the man fired from a job for holding an Eldridge Cleaver look-alike contest. This is the same guy who ripped the Russian flag from Rockefeller Center. So it wasn't fair to say that Imus discovered politics in the late 1980s and early 1990s, but he definitely put a stranglehold on it then.

It was August 2, 1990, when Saddam Hussein, the leader of Iraq, invaded Kuwait, seizing the country and its oil wells. Imus brought himself along for the ride. The program now featured interviews with politicos and talking heads. The comedy bits featured Hussein attacks that would continue even up through the nineties, when Rob would do Saddam singing "Iraq-a-rena," a takeoff on the popular song "Macarena."

As Imus continually says, he really only has guests on who interest him, with a few notable exceptions. Thus, with the Gulf War in the news and Imus already a news hawk and political junkie, it was natural that politics would become even more pronounced on the show than just the random sketch between records. On January 17, 1991, the morning after the troops were deployed, the *Imus in the Morning* program was all news. There wasn't much to laugh about that day. As the war rolled on, guests commenting on the war and an increase in the number of political guests enhanced Imus's legitimacy as a news source. It was during this time, and afterward, that he became of interest as a political outlet.

The revitalization of Imus, from getting clean and sober to having new playmates at a new station and reporting on the Gulf War, was clear. There was no better way to tell than the attention Imus was getting from his peers. In 1991 he received the National Association of Broadcasters Marconi Award for outstanding Major Market Personality of the Year. Not a bad way to celebrate the twentieth anniversary of your coming to New York.

# 9

# GOVERNOR IMUS AND OTHER STUPID-POLITICIAN TRICKS

They are the people who run our states and our country. Someone once said, "Washington is Hollywood for the ugly." True or not, we would submit that both politicians and movie stars have big egos, ripe for Imus's brand of puncturing. Though the Gulf War was over, politics on the Imus show kept on rocking. As each politician stepped up, like a deer in the headlights, Imus would head straight for him like a wild man in a Jeep Cherokee, waiting for him to run for cover or crash and burn. To wit . . .

It's easy to remember one of the biggest blunders by Vice President Dan Quayle. The VP was in New Jersey on the campaign trail in June 1992. Quayle, speaking to school kids, asked a young boy how to spell the word *potato*. William Figueroa recited P-O-T-A-T-O, and received a knock by Mr. Quayle for leaving an E off the end. What you might not remember is what happened to young Mr. Figueroa: He got a job with the I-Man.

Not as a producer or a writer; he was hired as a reporter. Young William had the responsibility of covering the 1992 Republican National Convention. For fifty dollars a day, he had to watch the event on television, then provide commentary on the event the next morning. It was a better deal than Figueroa got for the Democratic National Convention, when he delivered the Pledge of Allegiance. He may have felt more at home there, though, because Figueroa was a Clinton supporter.

Back to the early 1990s. Imus was settling in again. After he moved to WFAN, he bought a home in Fairfield, Connecticut. This wasn't the I-Man's first time living in the Constitution State. He had owned a home in Greenwich with Harriet and the girls. It was actually the Fairfield suburb of Southport where he was living now. Southport is a little community that is home to celebrities like Phil Donahue and Marlo Thomas; the queen of decorating, Martha Stewart; movie star Paul Newman; and NBC honcho Bob Wright. He was only a couple of towns over from friend Mike Lupica, who resided in New Canaan; Larry Kenney also lived in the general neighborhood. He shelled out an estimated $1.275 million for the house.

Instead of reveling in the problems of others, there was now plenty of time to revel in the agony of Imus and his new house. Imus would bitch about a light across the water from his home, which sat on a Long Island Sound inlet. At one point he suggested that he might just shoot it out himself.

There were also the seven hundred condoms. They were found in the septic tank of Imus's Southport mansion. He swore they didn't belong to him; Bernie thought they might be his lover's. Imus's reaction: He wouldn't ever sleep with anyone with AIDS.

He had mixed results with his Southport neighbors. Some loved him and would look forward to his weekly trip to the Spic 'n' Span market. Of course, they didn't live right by him, like an older woman named Thistle Hawkins. After she popped up on the Imus radar scope, he attacked with an invented Thistle Hawkins character. He liked some of the people, however, and was happy to talk about heading to the little market for the papers on Sunday morning or about how the locals would watch him when he came into town.

In those papers he picked up at the market, Don would soon discover that he was becoming a media darling in the state of Connecticut. It wasn't just the newspapers, either. Imus was profiled on a popular Connecticut Public Television sports program, *Talkin' Sports With Rod Michaud,* and featured in a big cover story in *Connecticut* magazine. The tease copy on the cover warned: "Imus! Lock the doors and hide your daughters. Here's the whole hideous truth about Connecticut's favorite morning madman." The magazine followed him in his Southport home, writing about his weekend there, and documented it with photographs. In Don's rebel fashion, one inside photo shows him wearing a T-shirt emblazoned with "Die Yuppie Scum."

The article did a terrific job of profiling Imus. A cast photo shows off the 1991 Imus crew (with the exception of Imus, of course). He is represented as a cardboard cutout. Pictures of his home show the Southwest style that Imus grew up with, and writer Andrew Marlatt even got Imus to admit the big bucks he was pulling in: twenty thousand dollars a year. Of course, not all the neighbors were happy to have Imus in town. One even threatened a lawsuit if his name was mentioned in the same article. Imus really brings out the best in people sometimes.

With all the attention he received, it was no surprise that Imus would start to follow the Connecticut news and begin to have on Connecticut guests. He made quick friends with Gov. Lowell P. Weicker. Weicker had been elected to the governor's chair of this staunchly Democratic state in a big three-way race in which he made it in as an Independent. It didn't hurt that Weicker had advertised and appeared on WFAN, which garnered huge ratings throughout the state of Connecticut.

Weicker repaid Imus with a big public-relations coup. He offered to make Imus governor of Connecticut for a day. Imus was practically salivating at the chance. For weeks he talked about what he would accomplish as governor. His first mission was to reinstate the death penalty in Connecticut and fire up "Old Sparky," the electric chair.

Before Imus could even get to Hartford, the Connecticut media gathered. Television reporters clamored for an audience with the I-Man, trying to win his favor and "backstage" access on the big day. The whole event brought about controversy from the Connecticut radio community. Why should a New York radio host get to be governor for a day? many competitive broadcasters asked. Some decided to ignore the story, some were jealous they didn't have the idea first, and others took a different government job. For example, a funny team on Hartford's WHCN, Picozzi and the Horn, used the day to trade jobs with garbagemen.

The day came, June 17, 1992 (not so coincidentally, the twentieth anniversary of the Watergate Hotel break-in). Imus didn't fail to mention this, either, digging out Larry Kenney's Richard Nixon voice to attack one of the men who, as a senator, had brought him down. "Sit on this, you fat bastard!" was the way the governor was welcomed. Imus didn't even receive many of the job's perks. For instance, he didn't sleep in the governor's mansion the night before but did say in honor of Watergate that they had broken into Weicker's office. The real governor seemed more concerned with what they might have left than what they had taken.

The day's event was actually a job swap. Lowell P. Weicker Jr. took his turn behind the microphone. The media stormed the location, *CBS This Morning* brought their cameras by for a live interview, and all the Connecticut stations sent reporters. There were political guests aplenty, with Vice President Dan Quayle, Senators Joe Lieberman and Al D'Amato, and even New Jersey's governor, James Florio, getting in on the fun. Quayle got slammed over the potato-spelling flap, which had happened the same week. Weicker "blew up" Lieberman for knocking him out of the Senate in 1988.

Meanwhile, Governor Imus had a plan for the state. After taking the oath of office, which included a pledge to raise every tax and take no bribe before his time, he announced his platform. Imus told those who inherited their wealth to find a job, made David Letterman's home a bed and breakfast, and dissolved all marriages between female newswomen in the state of Connecticut. He never did get to fire up Old Sparky, though. Maybe Imus is saving that for when he is president for a day.

Since Weicker ended up serving only one term, he was not much of a factor on the program after the governor-for-a-day bit. Having established Connecticut's first-ever income tax, he was not the most popular governor in the state's history. Weicker did pop up on the Imus radar during Connecticut's next election, 1994 to be exact. It seems that a friendly wager came about over who would be Lowell's successor, Weicker's lieutenant, Eunice S. Groark, or Cong. John Rowland. Imus took the congressman, while Lowell backed his second in command. It ended up with a thousand-dollar check to Imus, as the congressman nabbed the top spot.

To appear or not to appear; that may be the question when trying for an endorsement. Jim Florio appeared on Imus's show when he was running for governor of New Jersey. Despite the I-Man's endorsement, he lost the election. David Dinkins came on the show and nailed down the endorsement from Imus, but it was Rudy Giulani who ended up in Gracie Mansion. Geraldine Ferraro, while running for U.S. Senate didn't, and *New York Newsday* speculates that it may have cost her some votes. Clinton in 1992 was a big winner; Dole in 1996, not so big. So Imus's political clout comes and goes.

What's a radiothon? Similar to a telethon, similar to what Jerry Lewis does every Labor Day weekend, it's an on-air marathon fund-raiser for a particular cause. WFAN's radiothon began in 1990 as a major fund-raiser for the Tomorrow's Children's Fund (TCF), which aids children with cancer and their families. The focus of the radiothon expanded in 1994. Less than a year earlier, the general manager of WFAN, Joel Hollander, and his wife, Susan, lost a daughter to sudden infant death syndrome (SIDS). They created the CJ Foundation for SIDS to keep the memory of Carly Jenna alive and try to help find answers to this enigma.

The radiothon is much like any telethon. The radio station takes over the atrium at the World Financial Center for twenty-six hours in late winter, and all the WFAN talent appears, getting involved in the philanthropy. Each half-hour or hour is sponsored, and listeners are encouraged to call in and pledge. Why twenty-six hours? Well, that gives the big money-maker, John Donald Imus, two air shifts to bring in the funds. According to Imus, there has never been a radiothon as successful as the WFAN version. Actually, it's possible when you look at the numbers. The charities have counted on the over $1 million  raised every year since 1990, and in 1999 they took in over $2.5 million.

Not that even the radiothon didn't generate some controversy. In 1992, even though he was invited by WFAN, onetime talk-show host, then local reporter Gordon Elliott, was escorted from the stage by the cops. Imus was not going to consent to an interview on the air, even though Elliott sat himself down right by the I-Man. The misunderstanding did improve the take for the TCF, though. WNYW, Elliott's station, ran a 1-900 phone poll asking if Imus did the right thing, with the profits from the call going to the TCF.

Controversy can be the cause of the day any day on the Imus program, and sometimes he isn't even responsible for it. One man who can tell you about that better than anyone is the former junior senator from New York Alfonse D'Amato, who is probably still apologizing for something that happened in 1995.

It was the height of the O. J. Simpson criminal trial, and how the subject came up may remain a mystery, but Imus and D'Amato were chatting about it. What stunned even Imus was when the senator launched into an impression of Judge Lance Ito. He did the impression in pigeon English, and it was not an impression Rob Bartlett would be proud of. Imus, who likes nothing better than reveling in the agony of others, tried to stop him before it made the newspapers. The senator hammered the judge, saying Ito had trashed the legal system and loved being a star.

The damage had been done, and the backlash was severe. It made the cover of all the New York tabloids and headlines across the country. D'Amato, on the defensive, made a brief statement that hardly satisfied anyone. It almost took an act of Congress for D'Amato to finally, barely, climb out of the hole he had dug himself. He had to make a public apology on the floor of the U.S. Senate before the heat even dropped from boiling to simmer. Here's what D'Amato had to say, straight from the *Congressional Record:* "Mr. President, two mornings ago I gave a radio interview on the Imus talk-show program. I am here on the Senate floor to give a statement as it relates to that episode.

"It was a sorry episode. Mr. President. As an Italian American, I have a special responsibility to be sensitive to ethnic stereotyping. I fully recognize the insensitivity of my remarks about Judge Ito. My remarks were totally wrong and inappropriate. I know better. What I did was a poor attempt at humor. I am deeply sorry for the pain I have caused Judge Ito and others. I offer my sincere apologies."

Imus's power was once again felt on Capitol Hill. This

wouldn't be the last time, either. Almost a year after D'Amato put his foot in his mouth, Don Imus would do the same.

What other good people ended up saying bad things on Imus? New York governor George Pataki appeared in 1998 to attack the State University of New York at New Paltz for conducting sex conferences, which included an S & M gathering.

David Brinkley used an appearance on Imus to issue a mea culpa. In his last full-time appearance for ABC News, on election night in 1996, Brinkley had trashed incumbent president Bill Clinton as a bore. Even though he told Imus he was ashamed of his comment, he couldn't work any excitement up for Clinton, calling him merely "okay."

Sen. Joe Lieberman (D-Conn.) was outspoken on Imus about President Clinton's giving a national apology for slavery. Lieberman compared it to the Menendez brothers, convicted of slaying their parents, saying, "I'm sorry, Mom and Dad."

Step up and sign in, Roger Ailes. One might think that Ailes, one of Rush Limbaugh's partners and former president of CNBC cable, would know better before saying something on the air. Maybe not. In 1994 he attacked the Clinton White House, accusing them of hanky-panky in the Vincent Foster "suicide" case. That was just for starters. He went on to attack them for covering up documents in the Whitewater investigation and accused Clinton of trying to date ice-skater Nancy Kerrigan, saying, "She's the only one he hasn't hit on."

When the White House called NBC president Robert Wright to complain, CNBC said: "It was a joke. It's Don Imus." Just another example of bad things happening to good people. Keep listening; it's bound to be only a few days before the next shoe drops.

# 10
# IMUS ACROSS AMERICA

The broadcasting business was again going through a transition, particularly the radio side. As a result of deregulation, groups that were limited to a small number of stations were now only limited by the percentage of the service area they could dominate. (No group of stations could own more than eight stations, or 50 percent of any given radio market.) This gave a group by the name of Infinity a chance to buy a radio station that had been experiencing some success, WFAN in New York.

The person who brought this deal about was Mel Karmazin. Karmazin worked his way up from salesperson at WCBS-AM in New York to programming radio stations to station ownership. Within a few years he would supervise the entire CBS Radio group of stations, but first things first. Karmazin's ownership success in New York came thanks to his classic rock station, K-Rock, and an outrageous morning-show host named Howard Stern. Karmazin was the man who, along with Stern, would take a chance and do something different in morning radio and syndicate the Stern show—something of a landmark in the radio industry in 1988.

In the spring of 1992, another deal was cut, and the former ad salesman's company, Infinity, spent an estimated $70 million for WFAN, the all-sports radio station that included the talented Don Imus. One of Karmazin's first plans of action was to re-sign the I-Man. He tore up the last two years of the current deal that was paying Don an estimated $1.3 million. Imus's 1992 deal probably doubled his money, now paying him an estimated $3 million dollars. Karmazin also threw in a digital workstation, something the I-Man had been begging for off and on the air. All of which was a bargain when one considers that Imus's program may have had gross billings in the neighborhood of $14 million a year, just in New York business. Alone, the new contract started speculation in the business that Imus would go national.

One benefit of the deal Karmazin made with Imus was stock options, and plenty of them. The growth of Infinity Broadcasting as a company continued to make Imus an even wealthier man. Infinity had its battles with FCC regulators but it continued to grow at an amazing rate in broadcasting terms. In late 1997 the combined Infinity/Westinghouse/CBS Radio group grew to over 175 radio stations, thus making it one of the nation's biggest owners of radio stations.

In one month, June 1993, three new radio programs went national, thanks to the Unistar Radio Network. Two shows are based out of WJFK (a CBS Radio station) in Washington, D.C. Stations now had the chance to bring into their market the midday show of Watergate felon turned broadcaster G. Gordon Liddy. Liddy, you may recall, had masterminded several events that contributed to the fall of President Nixon. He went on to write several books before finding success on radio. Now he talks on issues of the day and advises listeners on any number of questions, including finding the best gun for home protection (a revolver).

In the afternoons, Don and Mike, "the Radio Gods," graced the airwaves. Don Geronimo (not his real name) and Mike O'Meara spend most of their time on locker-room-style talk, but don't make the mistake of thinking that means sports. Don and Mike's show is filled with phone calls from listeners, rating celebrities (Helen Hunt rates high with Don), and acting out games like "Strip Trivia" and "Low Budget Jeop-ar-dee." They share a studio with Liddy, also operating out of the nation's capital.

The third new program was broadcast live from a basement studio in Astoria, New York. *Imus in the Morning* was on "the bird" from 5:30 to 10:00 A.M. Eastern Time, though most stations carried it from 6 to 10 A.M. WQYK, in Tampa, Florida, came on the air as the first affiliate in the Imus network on June 14. This two-station team, WFAN being the flagship, would become five by the end of July.

Imus, like Paul Revere, would wake up Boston, thanks to WEEI. Imus would finally make it to FM as well, thanks to Providence, Rhode Island's WWRX-FM. As of this writing, all of these original stations are still proud Imus affiliates.

The newest listeners along the eastern seaboard started off hearing about, among other things, Imus's health regimen, a kick he had been on for years. He would run most days and talk about his trips to the health club. He was still a smoker, but after years of abusing his body, he was turning it around. Imus's life was now almost the polar opposite of the years of drug and alcohol abuse. Imus had spent the last few years working his way into a picture of health. His daily discussions would revolve around how far he ran; eight miles a day was not uncommon.

Imus would go on and on about running shoes. Expected regularly were reviews of various sneakers, pitting New Balance against Reebok or Nike. He was so psycho about his shoes, he ranted on one day because he could not find any with the right-colored stripe. He would go to work in bicycle shorts and even had a lifesized poster made of himself with bike shorts, sunglasses, and a baseball cap.

Despite all his exercise, Imus's body would eventually fail him. This time it was heredity instead of alcohol and cocaine. Just weeks after he started his national gig, he was struck ill. Imus's left lung collapsed. He ended up in Cornell University Medical Center. He knew the doctor well, though. Imus was under the care of Dr. Peter Guida, who may be better known in Imus circles as husband of longtime friend and guest Bernadette Castro. The lung would actually be reinflated and surgically attached to his chest.

Imus didn't want to lose a minute of his on-air time. Whereas years back he never would have blinked an eye at taking time off from work, his ethic had changed. After just a couple of days, he was phoning in reports from his hospital bed, which became a mixed blessing. While New York knew what to expect from the I-Man, these four new markets got to experience "The Best of Imus" and learn some of his background before they got used to his daily attacks. Maybe that is why those stations are still aboard and successful today.

Imus may have pushed himself too hard, though. Despite working his way back to the basement in Queens, a relapse landed him back in the hospital.

His new host of influential friends, especially those he had helped out, lined up to wish him better health. President Clinton passed along his good thoughts. Dan Rather sent his regards along with a cactus plant. (There is a prick joke here somewhere.) And speaking of pricks, at the head of the line to take cheap shots was Howard Stern, as usual.

Once he was back at work, Imus pushed himself on the air and off. He liked to show off his scars to the crew. He would initiate gruesome discussions on the air about running and reopening his wounds, then subjected poor Charles to the gory, bloody mess he had created. Imus worked to get off the painkillers his addictive personality wanted to get hooked on, too, sticking to Advil instead.

Stations kept joining the *Imus in the Morning* program, and from outside the big media markets. Now it was places like Portland, Maine, that were taking a chance with their morning shows, a time period that had been traditionally local. For good reason, "morning drive" is the most profitable portion of a station's day. Now stations were even paying for the privilege of touting the Imus name. Within the first three months, Imus was heard in ten markets across America. The deal to carry Imus on a station: a cash licensing fee and one minute of national commercials. In exchange, the station got about eighteen minutes of local time each hour (when Imus sticks to the format) and out of that, the first five minutes of the hour for local news and several other commercial breaks, including traffic and other local information.

The price tag was not cheap. Imus's program reportedly costs $1 million a year for some large-market stations and even $750,000 for Washington, D.C. It's an interesting problem for a station manager. One option for a station is the traditional route—paying for top-rank talent, plus health insurance and taxes, and other benefits they may have to include to attract them. The other choice is to buy the Imus show, which provides content 260 mornings a year, and write just one check. One has the benefit of having a local identity; the other, a proven national talent. It's a tough choice, but stations continue to choose *Imus in the Morning.*

The three programs launched in June combined to make 1993 what *Billboard* magazine would call "The Year of the Deal." In addition to Imus, Liddy, and Don and Mike, radio shows featuring talent with names like Moby, Donnie Simpson, Gerry House, "The Greaseman," Johnathon Brandmeier, Los Angeles's Mark and Brian, and even former *Partridge Family* star Danny Bonaduce premiered. Most had mixed results.

However, the name that people were talking about was not a radio personality but Mel Karmazin. Karmazin's Infinity had been managing Unistar, and he arranged a deal to merge with his biggest rival, Westwood One. According to *Broadcasting and Cable* magazine, the deal benefited Karmazin's Infinity to the tune of over $100 million and 25 percent of Westwood One's stock. Now names like Larry King and Jim Bohannon were under the same umbrella as Howard Stern and Don Imus.

Imus was looking very successful once the first set of ratings were announced. More surprisingly, since Imus had been in the hospital much of the time they were being counted. He was up in Boston, doubled the old numbers in Providence, and showed strongly on a weak station in D.C. As in New York, Imus was attracting a very key listener, upscale men twenty-five to fifty-four. These are the listeners whom advertisers clamor for, the ones who buy luxury cars, fancy running sneakers, premium beer, and other expensive items. Imus predicted that by October 1994 he would be heard in over fifty markets. Even the speculation that Imus might be coming to cities like Charlotte or Chicago sent reporters scribbling.

By June 1994, Imus was in over thirty markets around the country, not far off from the initial guess. It seemed to be a profitable partnership. After all, how can you expect to attract top talent like Imus to smaller markets like Spokane, Wichita, or Little Rock, which was the size of the market he was entering

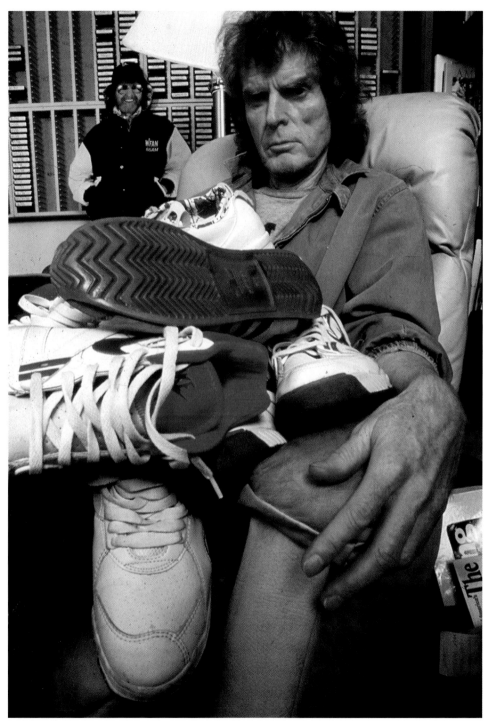

SNEAKERS CREEPERS  The I-Man doing his finest impression of Imelda Marcos, with a lapful of Nikes. (Photo courtesy © Todd France/Corbis)

SOMETIMES A CIGAR
IS JUST A CIGAR
Kinky Friedman, a.k.a.
The Texas Jewboy, at a
signing for his novel
*Armadillos and Old Lace.*
(Photo courtesy James
M. Kelly/Globe Photos,
Inc.)

SMIRKING IN THE
RAIN  The I-Man
walking between the
raindrops. He doesn't
look pleased. (Photo
courtesy Henry
McGee/Globe Photos,
Inc.)

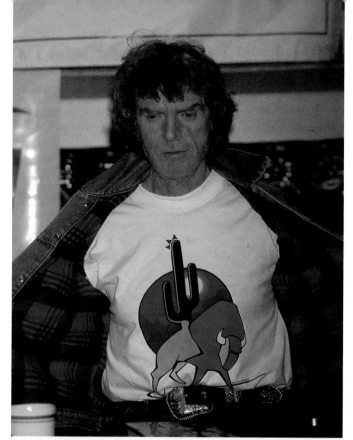

CACTUS MAKES PERFECT Imus at a signing for his best-selling book *God's Other Son.* (Photo courtesy Andrea Renault/Globe Photos, Inc.)

AND THEY SAID IT WOULD NEVER LAST Jesse Jackson and frequent Imus guest Tim Russert at the fiftieth anniversary bash for *Meet the Press.* (Photo courtesy James M. Kelly/Globe Photos, Inc.)

(*Left*) HOW GREEN WAS MY VALLEY  Imus guest Jeff Greenfield, at the Freedom Forum 1998 Robert F. Kennedy Book and Journalism Awards.  (Photo courtesy James M. Kelly/Globe Photos, Inc.)

(*Above*) NOT BAD FOR A BOY FROM TEXAS  The Kinkster (Friedman) at the National Medal of Arts and Charles Frankel Prize Dinner—at the one and only White House. (Photo courtesy James M. Kelly/Globe Photos, Inc.)

(*Left*) WRITER'S CRAMP  The I-Man doing the old John Hancock on a copy of *God's Other Son* at Waldenbooks. (Photo courtesy Andrea Renault/Globe Photos, Inc.)

TENNIS, ANYONE?  Imus at the 1996 U.S. Open, Flushing Meadow Park, Queens, New York. (Photo courtesy Andrea Renault/Globe Photos, Inc.)

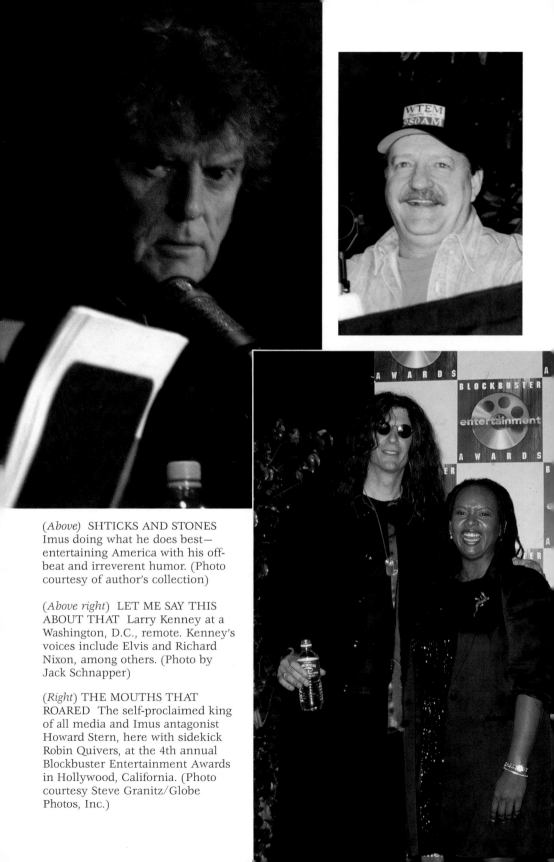

(*Above*) SHTICKS AND STONES Imus doing what he does best—entertaining America with his off-beat and irreverent humor. (Photo courtesy of author's collection)

(*Above right*) LET ME SAY THIS ABOUT THAT Larry Kenney at a Washington, D.C., remote. Kenney's voices include Elvis and Richard Nixon, among others. (Photo by Jack Schnapper)

(*Right*) THE MOUTHS THAT ROARED The self-proclaimed king of all media and Imus antagonist Howard Stern, here with sidekick Robin Quivers, at the 4th annual Blockbuster Entertainment Awards in Hollywood, California. (Photo courtesy Steve Granitz/Globe Photos, Inc.)

(*Above*) VA-VOOM! Imus regular Rob Bartlett with some of the ever-changing Bartlettes. (Photo by Jack Schnapper)

(*Left*) AIN'T SHE SWEET Deirdre Coleman-Imus (Mrs. Don) sits in during a Washington, D.C., remote. (Photo by Jack Schnapper)

SMALL IN THE SADDLE The I-Man looking characteristically grumpy at a 1998 personal appearance. (Photo by Jack Schnapper)

THE HARDEST WORKING MAN IN SHOW BUSINESS Imus producer Bernard McGuirk, famous for his Cardinal O'Connor character. (Photo by Jack Schnapper)

into. Profitable for the show, too. Overhead costs the same for two stations or two hundred. The distributor even rolled out a separate West Coast feed for stations in the Mountain and Pacific time zones. Now listeners could hear a tape delay of Imus from 5 to 9 A.M. on the Left Coast.

Two landmarks in Imus syndication occurred simultaneously. On July 1, 1996, as part of the influx of stations joining in the spring of 1996, Imus cracked the Top Ten in radio markets. Imus landed on KLAC in Los Angeles and now was heard in all of the Top Ten radio markets in the country. This is a benefit when trying to sell national advertising on the program, but since there is only a minute of national ads each hour, it didn't mean nearly as much as the prestige. Imus in Los Angeles also meant that he would get to compete for the first time, head-to-head, against Robert W. Morgan, his friend and mentor. KLAC was one of four other stations joining in early July. Imus was on in San Bernardino (KMEN) and in the east on WYST and WGMP. The Imus tote board now tallied eighty-five stations and counting.

Getting stations and keeping them are two different slices of the pie, however. Even for a town that had some Imus history, Cleveland, the "Mistake by the Lake." Imus joined his third station in Cleveland in September 1993. WWWE, known on the air as Three-W-E, signed the syndicated Imus show to a one-year deal at an estimated cost of between $20,000 and $250,000.

By February 1994 the Imus program on WWWE had experienced some ratings growth. Estimates showed about an 8 percent climb in listeners and a jump to eleventh place in the city's standings. Stern, meanwhile, also on in Cleveland, had almost four times the listeners. When August rolled around, WWWE did not renew Imus's contract.

The local paper, the Cleveland Plain Dealer, which once had a columnist try to get Imus fired, now helped spearhead a "Get Imus Back Campaign." They dumped on the station for not promoting Imus enough and called for another station to pick him up. In what has to be the most creative letter-writing campaign ever, writer Deborah Winston, along with a concerned listener, suggested not writing to Imus or WWWE or Westwood One. Instead, they said to send letters to Imus's buddies: Bob Dole, Bill Clinton, James Carville, Mary Matalin, Paul Begala, and even Four-Legged Fred, his brother's dog.

Was the Cleveland saga over? It will probably never be known whether the president intervened in this crisis in Ohio, but Imus did come back on the air. On Memorial Day, 1997, with a wait of only three years this time, Imus debuted on WKNR. If you're keeping track, the longest wait was between Cleveland II and Cleveland III (WHK to WWWE), about fourteen years. Between Cleveland I and II (WGAR to WHK) it was just seven years.

Unfortunately, the clock is ticking again, awaiting Cleveland V. It was early 1998 when Imus disappeared from WKNR. The company line was that Imus's ratings were still low. Interestingly enough, the switch coincided with the fact that the station had a new ownership. Jacor Communications, a competitor of CBS Radio, had their own shows to push.

Having their own radio shows to push may have been just the problem that WISN in Milwaukee had. The station designed an advertising campaign to promote the Imus program in their hometown. The ad took shots at disc jockeys on three other local stations. The problem was that WTMJ-TV, Channel 4, would not show the ad. Why, the station was asked by the *Milwaukee Journal Sentinel?* It didn't like running attack ads. One might guess that this would be especially true when one of the stations attacked was owned by the same company that owns WTMJ.

It was a school bus driver's insensitivity that really caught the eye of the I-Man, though. When an eight-year-old special-education student's mother complained about her son having to be subjected to the Imus show on his bus ride to school, she got no action from the driver or even the school's principal. So she moved her son across town to grandma's, effectively avoiding the bus, then took her case to the government. A complaint was filed with the Department of Human Rights, alleging sex and disability discrimination.

Even Imus was on Zachary Jacobs's side, saying the program was not what an eight-year-old should be listening to. The day the story hit the *Minneapolis Star Tribune,* school-district officials agreed, and Imus was off the air, at least on that school bus.

While the number of stations on the Imus network continued to grow behind the scenes, Imus could expand his guests as his listening audience grew larger. Now that Imus was heard in their constituents' hometowns, more politicians had an interest in showing off on Imus and getting the word back home.

Imus the interviewer had a knack of getting the most out of his interviews, be they politicos or celebrities. I-Man's subjects are varied and interesting. One day it might be a newspaper columnist, the next a television talking head, and the third a writer or a sportscaster. Imus will be the first to tell you that he selects only those guests who are the most interesting to him because he basically does the program for the benefit of himself. He will take suggestions from Fred and Bernie occasionally and is usually pleased with the results.

One memorable interview was with longtime New York Yankee turned Yankee broadcaster Phil Rizzuto. Imus and "the Scooter" chatted for a while about sports, something that is always on the I-Man's radar scope. The pair sidetracked into what might seem a strange topic, one most do not consider when thinking of legendary broadcaster Rizzuto. They talked about the Scooter's musical career.

Rizzuto contributed to a classic rock-and-roll song, Meat Loaf's "Paradise by the Dashboard Light." Rizzuto's voice is heard doing play-by-play while the song's characters are getting it on in the car. The play at second is close, he steals third, and then it's time to come home. Scooter's call is riveting, with the thundering music building to a crescendo in the background, "Here's the throw, here's the play at the plate. HOLY COW! I think he's gonna make it!"

Imus wanted to know what Rizzuto was thinking when he recorded the song. According to Rizzuto, he was just doing it as a favor, but he wondered why every play was a close one. He had almost forgotten about it when the song was finally released. Holy cow, he couldn't believe he had all the nuns mad at him! Rizzuto claimed he had no idea what his announcing talents were being used for.

Guests were finding out just how popular being on Imus was. Even realizing that they might have been better known for being on Imus than for anything else. Jeff Greenfield, now the CNN political guru, has often said that he has been stopped in the halls of the Capitol to talk about his latest broadcasting effort. Not because of the great piece he put together on *Nightline* the night before but for his appearances on Imus. Dan Rather, after a New York book signing, said over half the two hundred people he signed books for had heard him on Imus that same morning.

Most guests happily appear on the Imus show—except for maybe Al D'Amato, Roger Ailes, and . . . Well, you get the idea. No one is happier to be on Imus, or even mentioned on the program, than an author, and no one knows that more than Jane Mendlesohn.

What's nice about having your own radio show? Talking about whatever you feel like. Like talking about books that your wife likes. That's really all it was when Don mentioned *I Was Ameilia Earhart* by Jane Mendelsohn. Mrs. Don Imus, Deirdre, had been doing book shopping when she came across an unpublicized new novel. She breezed through the 145 pages and raved about it to her spouse.

Imus in turn raved about it to his listening audience, who went out and bought it in such numbers that it went into a second printing, jacking it up from 25,000 copies to 235,000, pushing it onto the *New York Times* bestseller list. So began the book clout of Imus in 1996.

So the story goes. It was actually Imus pushing his own book, *God's Other Son,* when it was rereleased in 1994 on audiotape, that had the publishing world take notice. It should have; it garnered a 1996 Grammy nomination for Best Spoken Comedy Album but was edged out by Jonathan Winters.

Imus used his clout again in 1997 when *Two Guys, Four Corners* came out, getting it onto the bestseller list. *Spin Cycle,*

Howard Kurtz's book on the Washington spin doctors, had Imus talking for days, and he even gave out advance copies of it on the air. That book went from a first printing in the tens of thousands to subsequent printings in the hundreds of thousands—another bestseller. Imus will tell you he has book clout that equals or surpasses Oprah Winfrey, who can put a book on the bestseller list with just a mention on her show.

What's the bottom line for the I-Man? The real benefit of being on across America? Selling books and Fred's shirts and salsa? The clout of having 15 million people listen each week? Possibly, but the best bet is money. There is a financial benefit from participating in the ownership of a radio giant and the rewards he reaps from the stock price. Probably even more important to the I-Man, he was carried on more and more new stations because Infinity stations would begin to carry programs from Infinity's syndication arm. This benefited not only Imus, but programs featuring Howard Stern, G. Gordon Liddy, and the stars of the *The Don and Mike Show.*

How does the class of June 1993 stack up today as far as stations are concerned? One of Liddy's station Web sites reports 232 stations, which beats the I-Man, who reports about 100, and Don and Mike announce they are on 60 stations (as of August 1998). It may not be fair to rate them in this manner, though, because they are all in different time periods and have different deals for their programs. However, being on 100 stations every morning, being heard from Bar Harbor, Maine, to Tacoma, Washington, and from Los Angeles to New York, is a feat even Howard Stern has yet to accomplish.

# 11
#####

# IMUS VERSUS STERN II—
# PAIN IN THE PLAINS

So with Imus and Stern both in syndication, radio's baddest
of bad boys mounted their steeds and readied to attack each
other on the airwaves across America.

The battle had never really stopped in New York, on and
on since 1985, though the seven years seemed to pass fairly
quietly (that is, if you can perceive that these two morning
mouths could ever be quiet). Stern had risen to the top at
WXRK in New York and was doing gangbuster numbers, from a
ratings perspective. It seemed to be all an executive could ask
for, having the number-one rated show in the biggest city in
America. Imus, even with lower ratings, seemed to garner
more prestige, though, for one simple reason: money. On Wall
Street and Madison Avenue, Imus seemed to be whom the
bosses were listening to. So even if two assistants for every boss
listened to Stern, the ad dollars went to Imus. They added up,
too. WFAN was soon number two to only Chicago's WGN in
billing, thanks to the *Imus in the Morning* program.

However, the psychological battle looks at the quantity of
people, not money, which brings about the "Legend of the
Dead Dog's Penis." It's true, around the time Stern was heading
for mornings, that Imus didn't believe that Stern could best
him. In fact, Imus said that if Howard Stern could top his ratings in the morning, he would eat a dead dog's penis. Once
Stern won the morning ratings race, both men commented on
the challenge. Imus said simply, "It tasted like chicken." Stern
felt bad for the poor dog.

While Stern still wins the New York ratings race on a regular basis, Imus is clearly the income winner. So is WFAN,

because it eventually passed WGN and has now set records in billing for several years running.

Just as one cannot talk about Imus and Stern at WNBC without mentioning Randy Bongarten, it's not possible to talk about the present-day big mouths without including Mel Karmazin. Having brought two of radio's biggest mouths under one cor-porate roof, Karmazin benefits from the success of both. Each time Howard Stern goes on a new station, his Westwood One network makes money. Each time Imus grabs a major new account, like the Jeep Eagle Sports Lock of the Week, coins end up in Karmazin's pocket.

You will rarely hear the boys (if you can call a forty-four-year-old and a fifty-eight-year-old boys) ever mention Kar-mazin, though. If they follow the rules, you won't hear his name at all. It is fairly well known that Karmazin placed a clause in both Imus's and Stern's contracts, forbidding them from talking about him on the air. Imus found a way around that, though, choosing to call Karmazin "the Zen Master," or by wearing an "I Love Mel" hat. He loves to throw his relationship with Karmazin around, too. He threatens to call the Zen Master about the crappy job CBS is doing to drive up the CBS stock above 50. (At one time it was above 35; currently it's in the high 20s from a low of 16 some years ago.) How much stock do they own? Imus says he owns "several million shares," and Stern doesn't talk about his finances at all. In the world of CBS Corp. it probably does not amount to much when you look at the whole pie. Karmazin's shares add up to around 2 percent of the total stock owned, so the boy's shares would likely be much lower.

Howard Stern deserves a lot of credit for pioneering the con-cept of syndicating a morning show on radio, thanks to Mel Karmazin's willingness to take the risk. Stern went on his Philadelphia station in 1988 and showed that the right mix of local news and national chat would work. He continued to bring in killer ratings in New York and whatever other cities he showed up in. He dominated those eighteen- to thirty-four-year-old listeners and drove up the score against the competition. He even started holding funerals for the competition he would top. One of the first took place in Philadelphia, where the local station he was burying even went so far as to try to get jackhammers to interrupt Stern's moment.

As successful as Howard Stern is in those cities in which he broadcasts, the "King of All Media" (his term) to this day has major difficulties getting new stations to air his program. By mid-1994, over five years after he started to go national, the Howard Stern program appeared in only seventeen markets, according to *Broadcasting and Cable.*

Stern must have been fuming, for once again he was sharing the spotlight with Imus. When Imus went national, he added five stations in the first month. Imus's landing in the hospital with his collapsed lung was the only thing Stern needed to attack. Stern could not have been more blunt when he sent his wishes to Don. "I hope he dies." Don lashed out at Stern's wife in retaliation.

It was no surprise that Stern had attacked his former coworker. He seems to just like to kick people at their lowest possible moments. He once waved a dead actress's ashes around the studio, another time playing a Selena song, accompanied by gunshots, after she died. Howard Stern had even wished death on the former chair of the FCC when he was struck with cancer.

Both Imus and Stern would have run-ins with the FCC. Pre-CBS days, Infinity Broadcasting wanted to add to their list of stations, an action that requires FCC approval. The commissioners of the FCC were dragging their feet, though, mostly because of Howard Stern.

Not long after Stern began in Philly, the FCC started to receive indecency complaints. After all, New York's tastes are one thing, but the community standards in Pennsylvania, outside the cradle of liberty, are different. Community standards are what the FCC relies on to decide an indecency complaint. One of Stern and Karmazin's biggest defenses was the old double standard: Oprah and Donahue said the word *penis* on their shows; why was it obscene on the Howard Stern show?

Stern ended up being fined by the FCC, in what Stern and

# Imus Versus Stern Timeline

| | |
|---|---|
| September 1982 | Stern starts at 66 WNBC—4–8 P.M. |
| 1983 | Stern suspended for "Virgin Mary Kong" Bit; Al Rosenberg begins working for Howard Stern as well as Imus. |
| 1983–85 | Positive cash flow at WNBC-AM |
| July 1983 | Randy Bongarten named general manager; moves Stern to 3–7 P.M. |
| Fall 1983 | "If We Weren't So Bad, We Wouldn't Be So Good" ad campaign premieres. |
| July 1984 | Bongarten promoted; leaves WNBC |
| September 1985 | Stern fired by WNBC; Al Rosenberg leaves WNBC to work full-time with Stern. |
| November 1985 | Stern starts at Infinity-owned WXRK in afternoons. |
| 1986 | General Electric buys RCA, including its subsidiary, NBC. |
| February 1986 | Stern moves to mornings. |
| August 1986 | Stern begins syndication on WYSP in Philadelphia. |
| July 1, 1987 | WFAN premieres in New York. |
| July 1987 | *God's Other Son* is rereleased. |
| August 1987 | Imus enters rehab center in Florida. |
| February 1988 | WNBC sale announced to Emmis Broadcasting |
| October 15, 1988 | WNBC signs off for final time. |
| October 18, 1988 | Imus's first regular broadcast on WFAN |
| January 5, 1992 | Infinity announces purchase of WFAN for estimated $70 million. |
| July 1993 | Imus begins syndication on Unistar Radio Network with three new stations in first month. |
| August 2, 1993 | Imus hospitalized for collapsed lung. Stern says, "I hope his other lung collapses." Imus verbally attacks Howard's wife. |
| October 1993 | Howard Stern releases *Private Parts*. |
| 1994 | Stern premiers on E! Entertainment television with half-hour show. |
| September 1996 | Imus premieres on MSNBC with three-hour show. |
| Fall 1996 | *Private Parts* movie released |
| Summer 1998 | Al Rosenberg rejoins *Imus in the Morning*. |
| August 1998 | *The Howard Stern Radio Show* premiers in television syndication, mostly on CBS-owned stations. |

Karmazin both considered a witch hunt. One example that would probably weigh heavily on their minds is that the initial FCC fine sanctioned only the Philadelphia station, even though the alleged obscene broadcast had aired both there and on New York's WXRK. They refused to pay the fines levied against them, and additional ones piled up. Piling *on* might be a better term, because at one point before the settlement, in just four findings the FCC had levied $1,678,250 worth of penalties against Stern and Infinity.

Karmazin continued to acquire stations, or attempted to. The FCC was slowing things down on the approval side; the regulators' implicit threat was that if Infinity didn't pay, it wouldn't get to play. In what was a rare moment of solidarity, Imus came to the defense of Mel Karmazin and Howard Stern. The statement would air live across the country in January 1994, on Imus's network of stations as well as on C-SPAN, the cable public affairs network. Imus did it with his own brand of humor.

First, Imus lashed out at the FCC, calling the delay in approving station sales "a power-abuse trip by a smug band of regulators who are a textbook example of what happens when you give tin badges to people who suffer a persistent sense of inadequacy."

Imus then defended Stern's right to say what he likes on the air. "No matter what puddle of putrescence he happens to be wallowing in at the moment . . ."

Of course, he also took a few smacks at Stern, almost incredulous that a First Amendment battle would come about over him: "This nitwit couldn't have distinguished the Bill of Rights from a utility bill until somebody pointed it out to him about twenty minutes ago."

He wrapped it up this way: "Stern is doing what he wants to do, I am doing what I want to do, Infinity Broadcasting should not be made to suffer in either case, and you should be able to listen to whatever you want.

"Coming up in a few minutes, I will be talking to Senator Bill Bradley, and Howard's going to have a lesbian stick a tent pole through her nipples. . . . Maybe I can tape it."

As valiant a defense as it might have been, Infinity Broadcasting ended up being the party that caved in first.. The settlement with the FCC after the piling on of complaints cost Infinity $1.7 million in fines against Stern's show.

The ever-present question remains: Did Imus steal Stern's ideas, or is Stern just Imus to the nth degree? There is no disputing the fact that in many ways Imus paved the way for the younger announcer. Imus was the first to write a book, though Stern's was an autobiography. Imus was governor of Connecticut for a day; Stern ran for governor of New York.

It was 1994, two years after Imus took over the reins of Connecticut's state government for a day, that Stern chose to run for New York's top job. He even secured the endorsement of one of New York's smaller political parties. Why isn't he working out of Albany today? He dropped out of the race for the seat so he didn't have to disclose his income, required of all political candidates. Was Stern worried that, in comparison, his salary was as small as he claims his penis is? Stern's salary has been estimated in the $2 million range; Imus's, $3 million. The world may never know for sure.

So since we have come down to the salary issue, let's debunk a couple of other myths perpetrated by Stern and his fans across the country.

**Myth:** WNBC was sold because Stern was fired and they couldn't make money.

**Fact:** As detailed earlier in the book, NBC was on its way out of the radio business, Stern or not. During the three years that Imus and Stern worked together for WNBC, the station made money. However, the main reason the stations were sold off was not due to a lack of profitability but the fact that General Electric had bought NBC. Under FCC regulations at the time, GE could not own both television and radio stations in the same market, so they sold off radio.

**Myth:** Stern has more lesbians on than Imus.

**Fact:** Imus once said he probably has on as many lesbians as Howard does; he just talks to them about their books.

**Myth:** Imus stole Stern's act.

**Fact:** In the statement he gave about the fines, Imus also addressed the issue of who stole whose act: "I did start all this shock-jock business back when it was novel. And for those of you that think Howard's act is the result of some nuevo creative genius, the facts are when he came here to New York from Washington, D.C., he was doing my act; obviously he had to come up with something else. And the tapes are available, by the way." You may also want to note that Stern even used the services of Al Rosenberg. Rosenberg had been one of Imus's writers and voices on the show for several years and made the jump to Stern around the time Stern left NBC. Rosenberg rejoined the Imus show in 1998.

**Myth:** Imus's MSNBC show is just a reaction to Stern's *E!* cable show.

**Fact:** While both of them are on television, that may be where the similarity ends. Both of Stern's television programs are taped and heavily edited before they reach the air. As it happens, Imus's program is done live every morning for three hours. Besides, *Imus Plus* was on television in the late seventies, before Stern even made it to New York.

**Myth:** Imus and Stern have shared a program director.

**Fact:** It's true, the poor guy! Mark Chernoff was once the program director at WXRK, supervising, among other things, *The Howard Stern Show.* He is now at WFAN lording over the I-Man. Imus harasses Chernoff, saying that he is too ready to attack his old coworkers. One thing about Chernoff: You will find him at WFAN early most mornings.

**Myth:** Imus is jealous of Stern's success.

**Fact:** Not if you hear him tell it. Imus encouraged his listeners to go see the movie *Private Parts.* When asked, Imus continues to say that he and Stern work for the same company, so when Stern does well, Imus does also.

**Myth:** Imus makes more than Stern.

**Fact:** To hear Imus tell it, he does. Imus and Stern will not go on the record about their salaries, and with good reason. Some reports have Stern making about $2 million a year and Imus $3 million. That doesn't count stock options, which they both have, though Imus may have more there, too.

One thing that may pay off for Stern is that the Zen Master is now a CBS big shot. Karmazin's power has given Stern the opportunity to have a nationally syndicated television program, with the backing of the CBS Eyemark Entertainment arm. Stern's show, *The Howard Stern Radio Show,* started on August 22, 1998, on about thirty-five stations in the United States and Canada, covering 70 percent of the country, and is designed to air against *Saturday Night Live* in most parts of America. The Saturday-night show is just like the *E!* program, a compilation of Stern's radio show, with a few additions. The show's premier ratings were low, according to an NBC press release. *The Howard Stern Radio Show* fell behind *Mad TV* and Roseanne's *Saturday Night Special.* The list of stations still carrying it continues to dwindle.

The one-on-one battle between Imus and Stern resumed in 1994. This time they were competing on Imus's playing field: politics. Since Imus had been successful in helping President Clinton and Governor Weicker get elected, the candidates for New Jersey's top job were both after an endorsement from him. The Republican, Christine Todd Whitman, and incumbent Democrat Jim Florio were both discussed on the Imus program. Florio got the nod. Imus was behind Florio because Imus thought Ms. Whitman was making empty promises to get elected. Don even said he would chauffeur Whitman around for a year if she won.

Howard Stern used an entirely different tactic to decide who got his endorsement. He took the first caller. Whitman's chief spokesperson was glad to have the free advertising. So Imus kept attacking Whitman, and Whitman attacked back, while Florio was glad to be on the I-Man's good side. When election day finally arrived, it was Whitman, the Republican challenger, who took the oath of office, leaving a little egg on the I-Man's face. Stern would get a much bigger payoff.

New Jersey is the best example of the public perception of Imus and Stern today. In Hackensack, you'll find a medical center named after the I-Man. The Don Imus/WFAN Pediatric Center for Tomorrow's Children is located at Hackensack University Medical Center, built with money raised on the radiothon. On the New Jersey Turnpike, you'll find the Howard Stern Rest Area. Or maybe you won't. Governor Whitman, in a payback for Stern's support in the 1992 election, named a public convenience after Stern. Unfortunately, one of Stern's fans tore down the sign.

# 12

# THE SPEECH FROM HELL

This chapter could also be entitled "Imus Versus Bubba" or "Stupid Politician Tricks, Presidential Style." After all, to just call it "The Speech From Hell" gives you the impression that it is just about that evening in March 1996. It really is about Imus and the most powerful man in the free world.

As has already been noted, by the early nineties politics was turning into Imus's bread and butter. Political guests were commonplace on the show now, with no thought given to having Sen. Bill Bradley or Bob Dole on the phone for a chat. However, one of the chief beneficiaries was now President William Jefferson Clinton.

During the New York primary in 1992, Imus was seemingly glad to hear from this southern presidential candidate. Paul Begala, a Clinton adviser (or in Imus's terms, "Clinton Butt-Boy"), was a fan, but says some of the campaign staff were worried it might not be the best idea in the world to have their candidate visiting a guy who called him "Bubba." Clinton's five-minute call to the program showed Imus that Clinton could dish it out as well as take it. Right at the top he told Imus that calling him Bubba was not a problem because "where I come from, Bubba's just another word for mensch."

Imus would have another chance to chat with Clinton before the election and quickly became a fan of the president's after election day. It also appears that Clinton became a fan of the I-Man's, to the point of keeping an Imus bobble-head doll on the desk in his study off the Oval Office. This didn't mean, however, that Imus changed his style at all. He was still playing bits that blasted the White House. Rob Bartlett had his Clinton impression down pat and would use it at any occasion. The Imus posse took shots at Bill and Hillary on a regular basis, even using characters like "Rush Limbaugh" singing "The First Lady Is a Tramp."

That didn't stop the president from appearing on *Imus in the Morning,* either. (What options did he have?) Here was a radio show with fifty or so affiliates and several million listeners that was broadcast in key cities like Washington, D.C., New York, and Boston and was actually fairly friendly to the administration. After all, the host did vote for him in 1992. Some of the other choices on radio, Rush, Stern, or G. Gordon Liddy, were probably his worst nightmare. So Clinton made the best out of an interesting situation and continued to support the Imus show.

Imus got the red-carpet treatment from the White House. Imus hosted President Clinton two more times on his program. First, there was an appearance to celebrate his first 100 days in office. Later, Clinton paid a visit to Imus over the telephone in February 1994. The interview, simulcast on the *Today* show, was designed to help further his health-care-reform agenda that was having a tough time across the country.

During the early 1994 health-care phone call, since he had the president's ear, right off the top Don complained. He said that when Mrs. Clinton had visited the same broadcasting complex Imus worked in to do *Sesame Street,* she had sent the Secret Service after him. Actually, he did chat with the president's wife about health care and how his lung operation had cost twenty thousand dollars. The president took the time to really put out his side of that issue before they moved on.

Apart from the initial interview on health care, it was anything goes, in the context of the conversation. Imus showed respect for the office, saying, "You know, you are the president, and I'm not going to ask you goofy questions."

Which lasted all of three questions, until this exchange, taken from the White House press records, occurred:

IMUS: Of course, I guess I could ask you—the bed in that old El Camino wasn't large enough to play football on; so, Mr. President, what was that Astroturf for? (*Laughter*)

THE PRESIDENT: You're old enough to remember what it was like with a pickup truck—nothing but metal in the back, right?

IMUS: Absolutely. (*Laughter*)

THE PRESIDENT: If you wanted to put—that's the only car I had then. I carried my luggage back there—it wasn't for what everybody thought it was for when I made the comment, I'll tell you that. I'm guilty of a lot of things, but I didn't ever do that. (*Laughter*) But I don't think I should disclaim it really—just leave it out there.

IMUS: I mean, it's like saying you didn't inhale, Mr. President. I mean, come on.

THE PRESIDENT: No, it's just that I didn't inhale in the back of the pickup. (*Laughter*)

They chatted about Saudi Arabia and Delbert McClinton; Imus asked Clinton about Whitewater, McCord talked about his vacation home in Arkansas. Even Bosnia and cholesterol were discussed. Overall, the president took all the questions and came out as a friendly, jovial guy who knew the answers.

Imus was becoming a legitimate political commentator in his own right. He scored an appearance on *This Week With David Brinkley* in March 1994, discussing Whitewater. Larry King would also grill Imus about Clinton in an interview. King would also work in a plug for the correspondents' dinner speech when Imus appeared on King's show less than a month before the event.

So the stage was set. On March 21, 1996, it was time for an up-close and personal edition of "Imus in Washington." He was asked to be the entertainment at the 52nd Radio-Television Correspondents Association's dinner, one of several that take place each spring in Washington. Another is the Gridiron Dinner, at which traditionally the White House lampoons itself; one could even find Nancy Reagan doing a song and dance for the media, behind closed doors. Imus knew of these media bashes. Just a couple of years earlier, he attended one as the guest of the *New York Times*.

This reception was open to the public, though, in a manner of speaking, on C-SPAN. The cable channel broadcast the festivities. They didn't know the shock they were in for.

The scene: a crowded White House ballroom filled with over three thousand people, the elite of the Washington media and politics. Speaker of the House Newt Gingrich graced the head table, along with the president, the first lady, and Walter Cronkite (the real one, not Larry Kenney). Since the head table seemed to seat more than the dugout at Yankee Stadium, let's just say that Imus sat near Mike McCurry at one point.

Out in the audience were politicians like Steve Forbes and media stars like Dan Rather, Sam Donaldson, and Peter Arnette. They were gathered in black tie and, having finished the meal, awaited the night's entertainment. They would not be disappointed, although it may not have been what they expected.

Walter Cronkite was the first to speak that evening, presenting an award on behalf of the correspondents' association. The veteran journalist is still well regarded by his peers and probably received the largest round of applause of the night.

Mr. Gingrich was next. The Georgia Republican was very quotable with his barbs that night. He may have wished later it had been true when he said, "We don't want to be judgmental this evening."

Still, he cast the first stone by taking a shot at Sam Donaldson. He then marveled at the fact that the three speakers were the Democratic president, the Republican speaker of the house, and the I-Man. "Of the three of us," Gingrich said, "you can pick someone you love, someone you hate, and still have time left over for something else."

He wrapped up by throwing one of Imus's famous bits back at him. "Neither the president nor I are going to censor your speech, but if you do say the wrong thing . . ." and the atomic-bomb sound effect went off.

The president then spoke and seemed excited to be the first person to welcome Walter Cronkite and Don Imus in the same sentence. He gave the master of ceremonies a heart attack when he said he had wanted to keep his speech short, then almost immediately said, "Thank you and good night."

As much as he had wanted to leave and go home to watch

his Arkansas Razorbacks play basketball, Clinton wasn't that desperate—yet. He went on and made jokes about his bumper-sticker slogan for his second-term campaign and generally kidded around. Then he made way for Imus.

Imus, very uptight in his tuxedo, stepped to the podium and began his speech with a question. Since Imus has often complained he was unfairly quoted on things and in order to comment on them better, here are some direct quotes from the C-SPAN broadcast:

> Thank you very much . . . um . . . this is kind of inter-esting; these don't appear to be my notes. . . . (You still have the folder I gave you? Where did this come from?) Well, nobody just leaves stuff like this just layin' around. . . . (*Laughter*)
>
> Heh, heh, heh . . . let me see if I can see what it says: "S. McDougall called again . . . says bank needs check and statement; told her both were in mail, ha ha ha. Jesus, she looks stupid in those tank tops." I think I'll just hang on to these. (*Laughter*)

The first joke actually seemed to go over pretty well. Cut-away shots of the first lady showed her giggling, though it was probably in reaction to the tank-top joke.

> Ah, here we go. Good evening Mr. President, Mrs. Clinton, honored guests, ladies and gentlemen, radio and TV scum.
>
> As you know, nearly every incident in the lives of the first family has been made worse by each and every person in this room of radio and television cor-respondents—even innocuous incidents. For example, when Cal Ripkin broke Lou Gehrig's consecutive-game record, the president was at Camden Yards doin' play-by-play on the radio with John Miller. Bobby Bonilla hit a double; we all heard the president in his obvious excitement holler, "Go, baby!" I remember comment-ing at the time, I bet that's not the first time he's said that. (*Turns to president*) Remember the Astroturf in the pickup? And my point is, there is an innocent event made sinister by some creep in the media.

The president and the crowd didn't seem to take this one as well. They hadn't turned on Imus yet, but the ice he was skating on was becoming dangerously thin. He kept them squirming on the dais with some Whitewater land-deal jokes, then set out to attack the rest of the room.

> When I was asked to speak here tonight and was told who would be in attendance, my initial thought was, Well, I've already said almost every awful thing you could say about almost everyone in the room. And then I thought, Well, almost everyone.
>
> Let's start at the bottom with you folks in the media and work our way up. Do you remember the infamous curbside shooting from the Vietnam War? Well, I'm watchin' the *CBS Evening News* with Dan Rather and Connie Chung, and things are not going well, and I'm thinking we're a couple a nights away from another hideous photograph. I mean, everybody knows Dan Rather is capable of anything, including pulling a gun out on the set of the *CBS Evening News*. . . . Watchin' Dan Rather do the news, he looks like he's making a hostage tape. (*Laughter*) They should have guys in ski masks and AK-47s just standin' off to—
>
> By the way, nobody wants us out of Bosnia more than Tom Brokaw does. Just so he doesn't have to pronounce Slobodan Milosevic. . . . and we know Brian Williams is standing in front of the White House, thinking, I'm two Serb war criminal names away from Tom Brokaw's job. (*Laughter*)

Even these two media attack jokes went well. Dan Rather, always a big fan of Don Imus's, was laughing right along with everyone else. Then, like a school of sharks smelling blood in the water, the crowd turned for good on Imus, all because of a Peter Jennings joke.

> And then there's Peter Jennings, who we are told more Americans get their news from than anyone else—and a man who freely admits that he cannot resist women. So I'm thinking, Here's Peter Jennings

sitting there each evening, elegant, erudite, refined. And I'm thinking, What's under his desk? I mean, besides an intern. (*Groans*)

By the way, and this is really awful (*Laughter*), if you're Peter Jennings and you're telling more Americans than anyone else what's going on in the world, shouldn't you at least have had a clue that your wife was over at Richard Cohen's house? (*Laughter, groans, boos*) She wasn't at my house!

It seemed it was all over for the I-Man now. The sweat was noticeably pouring off him, making him shine under the klieg lights. He finished off Bernard Shaw and continued on to the Sunday-morning shows, comparing veteran journalist David Brinkley to E.T. Then he attacked the rest of the Sunday pundits:

There's also Sam Donaldson and George Will. Sam, the New Mexico sheep rancher— You would think that anybody who's taken as much money from the government in wool subsidies as he has could come up with something better to put on his head. I mean, what is that? (*Laughter*)

*Meet the Press*, with the utterly charming and gregarious Tim Russert, has brought a new sense of adventure and enthusiasm to Sunday-morning television. Mr. Russert's unique and probing interrogation of guests is widely seen as bold and refreshing. Sawing off Bob Kerry's wooden leg was a special moment.

And Ed Bradley: rethink the earring thing. Ed, you're a newsman, not a pirate. (*Laughter*)

Don't think Cokie Roberts, Mary McGrory, William Safire, and Mike Wallace missed out on the jabs, either. Wallace was there in person to take his lumps, while the I-Man pressed on and attacked those in the press who spend their days covering 1600 Pennsylvania Avenue.

The White House press corps— I mean, no wonder the president doesn't want to hold any news conferences. Who needs to be assaulted by a pack of rodents whose idea of a question is to confront the president with an insulting observation designed to impress their equally rude and arrogant colleagues: "Mr. President, Rita Braver, CBS News. We all know you're a pot-smokin' weasel, that you once ate an apple fritter the size of a baby's head, that you actually run a twelve-minute mile. Can you, therefore, tell the American people why that thing on your lip looks like a Milk Dud, and if it is a Milk Dud, and I'd like a follow-up." "Sir, Brit Hume, ABC News. Sir, everybody knows the closest you ever came to standing in a chow line was the cheeseburger window at McDonald's. So tell the American people, is that where you came up with 'buy one, get one free'?"

The president gets treated better by Rush Limbaugh.

Imus also made sure he spent plenty of time on the elected officials, too, dishing out lumps to the rest of Washington. It almost seemed that Imus's AK-47 brand of comedy was trying to ensure that it mowed down as many targets as possible.

And it was Newt, remember, who wanted to give every kid mired in the poverty of urban America a laptop computer. Not nearly as popular as Phil Gramm's plan to give every white male in the country a lap dancer.

And I agree with Ted Koppel. Pat Buchanan has a certain inherent charm. However, if he gets elected president, two weeks later somebody's going to come knockin' on the door at three o'clock in the morning: "Just checking. What kind of a name is Imus?" Although all this stuff about Pat Buchanan being anti-Semitic, I don't know about that. A lot of people aren't aware that he lost a relative in the concentration camps. His uncle fell out of a guard tower.

The audience may have been coming back around after a while, the Jennings jab almost forgotten by the time he hit everyone with the guard-tower joke. A few laughers were still seen in the audience scattered around, but for the most part, it was as quiet as a bad sitcom with no laugh track.

> In fact, as you know, Senator Dodd has recovered sufficiently to become the general chairman of the Democratic National Committee and will play a pivotal role in the president's reelection efforts. In fact, he has a couple of bumper-sticker ideas: "Clinton/Gore Please Raise Your Right Hand." Or perhaps, "Clinton/Gore/Four More . . . or Five to Ten." Now we're not sure what role James Carville or his dog will play in all this, but isn't it just like a Democratic consultant to come along and make a mess and then expect somebody else to clean it up.

Believe it or not, Imus did try to wrap up his message in a mostly kind way.

> One of the things that it seems to me that the media ought to think about in the coming months, particularly in this election year, consumed by the chaos of the campaign, is the sensibilities of the people you are covering. The way you cover them and your treatment of them as individuals. For if nothing else, they are all good and decent people who, for whatever reason, have chosen to devote the bulk of their adult lives to public service. People who possess a passion for ideas and ideals to which they have committed extraordinary energy. It is almost always irrelevant and short-sighted to seize only on the unfortunate human imperfections of people who frankly have demonstrated an often puzzling willingness to endure great sacrifice, both personally and professionally, for what they see as a noble summons to serve the greater good. More often than not, however, that is exactly the case. You folks focus on each misstep, every misspoken word, each testy outburst. Do they not deserve some degree of our respect? To be treated with the dignity that at least acknowledges the mission of altruism they believe they're conduct-

ing. Shouldn't we be willing to give them some benefit of the doubt?

I don't think so.

Thank you all very much.

Imus did not have to wait long for a reaction to the speech.
The first real warning of major problems was the silence he
faced during most of the speech, along with the groans and boos
that accompanied it. It would get worse before it got better.

At his daily press briefing on Friday, March 22, 1996, press
secretary Mike McCurry would have to deal with the "Imus
issue." Taken directly from the on-line archives of the White
House are some selected comments Mr. McCurry made about
the previous night:

> Mr. McCurry: I haven't had an opportunity to talk to
> the president and the first lady about last night's enter-
> tainment because they fled the scene as quickly as
> they could. I cannot attest whether that was due to
> the lack of quality of the entertainment programming
> or whether it was more likely due to the basketball
> game that was televised last evening involving the
> president's alma mater. I believe that a large part of
> that—I personally believe a large part of that enter-
> tainment—that's what we call it—offered last night was
> fairly tasteless, and I didn't know whether young chil-
> dren ought to be subjected to it, courtesy of C-SPAN.
>
> I called Susan Swain down at C-SPAN and said,
> "Look, before you guys reair this just think about
> whether you think that's something that ought to
> be on the air." I have no idea what their reaction to
> that was.

C-SPAN would go on to rebroadcast the speech no less
than six times over the weekend and still, in fact, makes copies
of it available for a modest fee. The press would continue to
grill McCurry on censorship.

> McCurry: I'm sure there are many people, especially
> on certain parts of Capitol Hill, that do find it offen-
> sive. But I don't. If anyone wants to compare that to
> the program last night, go ahead and try.

But then he got back around to other questions:

Q: If you can't speak for the family, was there wide-spread agreement among White House aides that were present that the program was in bad taste?

McCURRY: I think that there was about 99.9 percent agreement of most of those in attendance that it wasn't a compelling event that reflected well on any of the participants. . . . I had plenty of people there last night come up to me and not only apologize and ask me to express to the president their sense of regret at the nature of that performance, but I had a lot of people sort of indicate to me that they didn't think the president should have to sit through that kind of thing again.

Q: Absent asking him his personal views, do you know enough to be able to characterize the president's view of last night?

McCURRY: No. He left and went home. He watched the basketball game, and I think he was probably a lot happier doing that than he was sitting there.

Q: Did you think about leaving in the middle of it?

McCURRY: I did. In fact, the reporter I was sitting next to suggested that we all ought to get up and walk out, and it was not a bad idea, and I was getting prepared to send a note down the table saying, "Let's go," when, mercifully, it came to an end.

Q: But he likes Imus, doesn't he? He's been on his program.

McCURRY: Not in quite a while.

Q: Wait a minute. Is that a matter taste, or is that just a matter of circumstance?

McCURRY: Say again?

Q: Is that because—

McCURRY: I don't know, Brit. I was not here when he— He apparently was a long time ago on it, but I wasn't here then.

By my count, over thirty different articles were written on the subject, most condemning Imus for his indiscretion. *U.S. News & World Report*'s April 1, 1996, headline read "A Bomb Goes Off in the Nation's Capitol," and followed by: "Bill Clinton should have stayed home and watched his Arkansas Razorbacks compete for the NCAA basketball title." "An audience of 3,000 endured a big-time dud." "As for the president, he was clearly not amused."

*People Weekly*'s April 8, 1996, headline read: "TOASTED: Don Imus's dinner shtick brings travail to the Chief" and got quotations from the guests. Cokie Roberts, a frequent guest on Imus's syndicated radio show, said he "went way, way, way over the line." Wolf Blitzer, from CNN, told of the president's reaction. "I've seen that look before; if you could kill, that's the look you would give." Sam Donaldson of ABC was an Imus defender, though: "Don Imus did what Don Imus does."

This seemed to be the reaction from Imus himself. *People* asked the I-Man if he would apologize to the Clintons. "I don't *think* so. I let 'em off the hook! What the president needs is a sense of humor, and so does she."

Even before that interview went into print, a strange set of circumstances had CBS News's legendary newsmagazine program *60 Minutes* working on a profile of Imus. It hit the air just ten days following the speech. The piece, which was your basic *60 Minutes* profile, now had a real hook: They had a presidential insulter on tape and had the first interview with him after the fact.

Mike Wallace was the reporter, and in the middle of the piece he even admits to being a fan of the program. He also drops the hammer on Don for the racist humor of the program. Charles McCord and Bernard McGuirk are also interviewed, and it's McCord who defends his boss, reminding Mr. Wallace that no one is safe on the program, especially Mr. Imus.

The *60 Minutes* piece aired twice, once in March 1996 and then edited and repeated in the summer of 1998. The second, slightly longer version delved even more into the race issue. In fact, in the added snippet, Imus is caught by Mr. Wallace trying to deny saying that producer Bernard McGuirk's job is to "make nigger jokes." Imus went on to say he doesn't think anyone who really listens to the show thinks he's a racist.

Returning to Clinton, Imus takes time to defend himself. In a clip from the radio show played on *60 Minutes,* Imus believes he did okay in D.C. "They invited me down there to do what I do, and I did it. And now they say they're shocked? They owe me an apology. . . ."

Imus has credited several people, especially James Carville, for standing behind him when the press attacked. This seems especially loyal of Carville after being on the receiving end of one of the Speech From Hell's jokes. He also took steps to admonish people from the program who attacked him after. Most notably, Cokie Roberts earned a "lifetime ban."

Don't believe that Imus thinks the speech was perfect, though. Mostly, he says he was "comfortable" with it, having worked on it for more than six weeks before delivering it. He knew he was headed for a crash and burn and claims he was bathed in "flop-sweat." Of course, that gave Stern and his fans another chance to kick Imus. One Stern fan's Web page offered "pint-sized containers (of flop-sweat) bearing the likeness of Howard Stern, King of All Media, spanking Imus savagely." Imus did say that he would "never apologize" and has held that position to this day.

While it might have affected Clinton in a negative way or at least portrayed some of the stuffier members of the inside-the-beltway media in the wrong light, it certainly had benefits for Imus. In less than a month, Imus was back in *Time* magazine, as a winner! "DON IMUS Unburnt by his toasting of the First Family, he is inducted into the Broadcasting Hall of Fame."

In late April 1996, Don Imus would travel to Las Vegas, the site of the National Association of Broadcasters (NAB) yearly convention, most definitely the largest of all the broadcasting organizations. There he would join the ranks of entertainers like George Burns, Arthur Godfrey, and Edward R. Murrow as an addition to the NAB Hall of Fame. Imus was the only person inducted in 1996 and only the fiftieth radio inductee in the Hall's twenty years of existence.

If you think it's hard to get into the Radio Hall of Fame, it is. It's so exclusive that Guglielmo Marconi, the man credited with *inventing* radio, didn't even make it into the hall in its first year as an organization.

The radio side of Imus most definitely benefited from the speech. All of the media coverage garnered by the event earned Imus new recognition among listeners. WFAN reports that twenty new stations "immediately" signed up to carry the *Imus in the Morning* program. By September, Imus would also be back on cable, and what may have been the best kudo was yet to come.

# 13
#####

# BACK ON CABLE

**B**y late 1996, there were fewer people on radio with more reach than Imus. His stature grew with each station added, and he ranked as one of the Top Five most-listened-to personalities in radio. He was now known as a famous presidential insulter. He was a living legend, in the Radio Hall of Fame, while he continued to broadcast. He had a 100-station network of affiliates, something unprecedented for a morning show. He had sold hundreds of thousands of books, showcasing his clout in the publishing world. He was a natural for television.

Imus had become a semiregular fixture on C-SPAN, the cable outlet better known for televising Congress live. While things at the Capitol were slow, they would bring their cameras into Imus's Astoria studios as well as to other morning shows around the country, but more frequently Imus's. It was enjoyable to watch, simply for the ability to see what happened when the radio program was airing commercials. Usually, it was just Imus calling Deirdre, chewing gum, or chatting with McCord, and sometimes it was very tedious. Call it interesting in the voyeuristic sense or maybe just in the sense of slowing down to look at a car wreck. In one of his C-SPAN appearances, Imus actually defended Howard Stern and his boss Mel Karmazin. Imus had other occasional appearances on television as well. He was on *Nightline* with candidate Clinton, later simulcasting on the *Today* show with the president. Don't forget the CBS connection, either. He had several appearances on the old CBS *This Morning With Harry Smith and Paula Zahn*. He even yucked it up with David Letterman and has taken tons of questions from his friends Larry King and Tim Russert.

Even *Time* magazine had its eye on the I-Man, giving him the chance, along with a few other celebrities, to offer President Clinton some advice for the second term. Jay Leno thought Clinton might want to avoid the conflict of interest of prison reform. Imus's advice was similar and short and sweet. "I'd read him his Miranda rights."

It's hard to know exactly why MSNBC wanted to carry Imus. In one respect, the NBC affiliates did not want another version of *Today*, in whatever form, competing against their number-one network program on MSNBC. Therefore, traditional news was not an option. Though with people rising in the morning, repeats of *Time and Again* might not satisfy what MSNBC viewers were looking for. Plus, it would not hurt to have something already known that could generate its own audience start off the mornings. Imus seemed like a good fit.

Imus says that he has had conversations with CNN and ABC News about being part of their cable operations as well. It's not surprising that they are interested. While national ratings are hard to come by for MSNBC, Imus revels in the fact that they have beaten CNN five to one in New York, and are strong in Washington, D.C. Imus also revels in the fact that—as he tells it, anyway—he makes more money from MSNBC than Microsoft chairman Bill Gates.

For the fans who had the chance to watch the C-SPAN broadcasts, the first reaction was that of joy. However, the reality was that MSNBC is commercial broadcasting and would actually like to make some money on the program, so they air commercials. Which means that most of the intercommercial chatter was lost. In the beginning, some of the program was lost as well. It was difficult to coordinate the MSNBC commercials with the radio commercials. A rigid television format called for MSNBC to break at twenty-six after the hour, every hour, for local news from its affiliate partners. Imus would continue on with his radio program, and portions were taped for later broadcast, if there was time. That would mean that if you were watching MSNBC, you might see the first segment of sports, then the last when you came back from the MSNBC news and commercial break, and then the middle portion when the radio program went to a commercial. Confusing, to say the least.

To the credit of MSNBC, the two shows run seamlessly

now. The local news now runs in the radio's local news break at the top of the hour. Sports reports are not hopelessly chopped up, either. The biggest challenge for MSNBC now is the commercial disparity. The radio program actually allows for about four more minutes of ad time than the television program. MSNBC fills the time well, though, with "flashbacks" to previous programs and preproduced inserts, like the adventures of "Mark From Milwaukee" or the "Imus Dance Party."

As much as Imus says that he is doing a radio show, not a television program, there is some excellent television going on around him. The MSNBC gang is as creative as its counterpart over in Astoria. MSNBC has produced some great and interesting visual comedy. During one Imus vacation, a "Best of Imus" program featured "Pop-up Imus," a takeoff on the VH-1 show. The crew routinely goes behind the scenes with Rob Bartlett at his stage shows and produces hilarious segments from the taping. Crew members have followed Delbert McClinton at his concerts and spent time at the ranch to bring us a look at what will happen to the 810 acres.

The critics have noticed what a great job everyone on *Imus* has done to make the radio-on-TV project work. The *New York Observer* gave it rave reviews, and so did Fraiser Moore, television critic for the Associated Press. Since opinions are like belly buttons, meaning everyone has one, here's one from the negative side. Former *TV Guide* critic Jeff Jarvis, an admitted Stern fan, weighed in against the show.

Don't think for a moment that everything always goes easy for MSNBC. Imus has taped over the camera lenses several times. Once was just so he could "allegedly" eat chicken wings without Deirdre seeing. The one "blackout" that really stands out is the battle Imus had with MSNBC's media-relations department.

When Maria Battaglia made the comment that Keith Olberman and Brian Williams both surpassed Imus's MSNBC ratings, the investigation was on. Imus found the real numbers, and once he determined more people watched *Imus on MSNBC* than the evening guys, he lashed out at the spokeswoman, who was now called Maria "Buttafuco." The following day, after Imus still could not be placated by MSNBC executives, he taped over the cameras.

Not long after the Imus premiere on MSNBC, now being seen as well as heard across the country, *Time* magazine took another look at John Donald Imus Jr. Despite his huge network of media people that appear on the show, it was actually when Imus appeared on PBS's *Charlie Rose* show that he found out why. Rose spilled the beans that Don was in one of the final cuts of making *Time* magazine's 25 Most Influential Americans of 1997. Imus reacted almost passively at the suggestion, thinking cynically that someone at *Time* probably had a book to push.

The actual announcement came just a couple of days later. Not only was Imus named in the Top Twenty-Five; he graced the lower right corner of the cover, sharing the front page with people like TV hostess Rosie O'Donnell and cartoon character Dilbert. Inside, Imus received about three-fifths of two pages, the remainder going to, of all people, frequent Imus guest John Kerry. Actually, the article on Imus was one simple, non-earth-shattering column and a bizarre picture of the I-Man in an orange jumpsuit that one might find on Charles Manson. Five Marconi Awards and being in the Radio Hall of Fame were nothing in the mind of Imus compared to being one of the 25 Most Influential Americans.

Imus took his well-deserved honor and gave it a test-drive a few weeks later on *Larry King Live.* One of the first things Imus did to King, with whom he has been friends for many years, was just stick it right in King's face. He told King how he had to be jealous that *he* was in the *Time* 25 and King was not. King's claim that he belonged in the International 25 was a lame comeback at best.

Why didn't *Time* pick Howard Stern or even Rush Limbaugh as their radio person in the Top 25? They both have more listeners, but do either have clout? Look at Limbaugh's clout. It is strictly Republican, or conservative. Imus can have the head of the Democratic National Committee on one day and Bob Dole on the next. Stern may be able to get people to call in and say "ba-ba-booey," but can he get millions of dollars to build a hospital building for sick kids?

While Imus might have been associated with some of the other winners, like Dr. Andrew Weil and Trent Resnor, by being on the same list, that didn't mean Imus actually wanted to associate with them. He labeled a party thrown by one of the selectees to get all of the Top Twenty-Five together as ridiculous and railed against them several times on the air. After this, and the Greenfield invitation raffle, some sound advice to all is this: Don't invite Imus to anything.

Some of the most entertaining episodes of the Imus show are the remotes. Imus has traveled around the country to visit his local radio affiliates. Along the way, he has brought both controversy and humor. You never quite know what's going to happen—from meeting old acquaintances to facing off with a mayor or even making faces at an author. Remote time is the time to expect the unexpected.

**Dateline: Washington, D.C.** Remember Lyndon Abel, the nineteen-year-old responsible for producing the program after Imus's return to NBC in 1979? Well, when the former producer, now in his thirties, heard that the I-Man was coming to his D.C. affiliate for a remote, he decided to pay a visit to his former boss. Abel's job during the early 1980s had largely been to make sure Imus showed up once he started drinking and drugging again. When Imus spotted Abel through the glass of the control room, instead of a warm reception, he hammered the past producer, saying what he *had* produced was drugs. Seems a shame to attack the poor guy like that; maybe he had it coming, or maybe Imus just didn't like the memories associated with him.

**Dateline: Scottsdale, Arizona.** Not long after Imus joined MSNBC, on Halloween night, 1996, Imus hosted the Hate Radio Rodeo. Think of it as the Kramer reality tour for Imus fans, a five-day gathering of Imus-related fun. The group, over six hundred strong, holed up in the Princess Resort Hotel in Scottsdale, Arizona. The Halloween-night dance and party featuring Delbert McClinton rocked. Rumor has it a fan might have spotted the Imus family in the crowd on occasion.

Even though the hours were late the night before, the crew was ready on All Saints' Day morning (that's November 1) for a great show. Delbert and his band played an early-morning—5 or 6 A.M. local time—gig. Quite a few fans have been holding out for a repeat, but so far it's the original and the only official fan gathering.

**Dateline: Bangor, Maine.** What may have been the most controversial remote (to date) would be the trip to Bangor, Maine, which exploded onto the pages of the local newspaper months before Imus would arrive in town.

You really need to know about three people to understand the controversy. Imus should be very familiar by this time. The second is the brainchild of the promotional idea. Martha Dudman is one of the owners of WWMJ, a highly rated oldies station based in a small town just outside Bangor. Dudman is a very smart former president of the Maine Association of Broadcasters and a well-respected woman both in the community and the state. The third body in this triangle of hell was the mayor of Bangor at the time, Patricia Blanchette. Blanchette is a part-time mayor and full-time bookkeeper for a large chain of Maine grocery stores.

At the end of Main Street, as you come into Bangor, stands the Civic Center. In front, as a symbol of the logging and paper industries that helped make Bangor big, is a statue of Paul Bunyan, from the famous children's tales. Just the base of the likeness of Bunyan towers ten feet off the ground, so you know it's a big statue. Every few years, when the Shriners came to town to celebrate, the statue of Bunyon was adorned with a giant red fez, the symbol of Shriners everywhere. This gave Dudman an idea. If the Shriners can be saluted by placing a fez on Paul's head, then the I-Man should be saluted by placing an Auto Body Express shirt on the giant statue.

This request was presented to the city council. Let's say it was not greeted with open arms. In the days following, the *Bangor Daily News* documented the minutes of the meeting, and within a few minutes after starting the program, a copy of the article was in the hands of Don Imus.

The I-Man was not shy about launching into the attacks. Dudman was trashed for the idea in the first place. The mayor also took a few shots for complimenting the Shriners while not even acknowledging the work Imus has done for kids. The reporter, Roxanne Moore-Saucier, was probably hit the hardest for, in Don's opinion, not trying hard enough to get a quote from him.

The city council eventually had to make a decision, and they decided against Imus. A new local ordinance was passed not allowing any decoration of any statue in Bangor, Maine. Even the Shriners were held to the new standard, with the giant fez now sitting between the giant lumberjack's legs instead of on his head.

Imus arrived in Bangor to a packed Civic Center. The center that has hosted state-fair exhibits and even a movie premiere now packed them in for a radio guy. Imus welcomed the mayor on the show, and they traded barbs. The mayor was on the offense from the beginning and lashed out at Imus for comments he made about her. She came with gifts, too; in addition to the traditional key to the city, Imus got a set of moose-dropping earrings.

The real benefactor of Imus's visit to Bangor wasn't the city council or the radio station but a little-known camp. Like many of the road shows Imus does, the Bangor appearance raised funds for a local charity. Bangor's benefactor was United Cerebral Palsy's (UCP) Camp CaPella. Camp CaPella sits on a small lake about fifteen miles outside the city. The totally handicapped-accessible camp gives UCP of northeastern Maine's kids a chance to have experiences they might normally miss out on. The $6,600 will go a long way helping kids be kids.

**Dateline: New Jersey.** The event was not the program on remote but Imus accepting a challenge. Imus would rail against golf on the program—how easy it was and what a chump sport it was. As a result, he was called on the carpet by AT&T. The company challenged Imus to one hole of golf to benefit the Tomorrow's Children's Fund. Just one hole—with a catch. Imus started off with a pool of $50,000 he could win, but for every stroke over the par 5, the pool would drop $5,000. Imus took the challenge seriously. He acquired some of the best golf clubs available and went out and practiced his swing with a golf pro. To add the Imus touch, he commissioned a special pair of golf shoes. Golf cowboy boots, actually, with the little metal spikes in the bottom.

With his coach Bob Gelb from the *Mike and the Mad Dog* program at his side, on September 22, 1997, Imus took to the course. Looking like a deranged preppie, Imus had on a blue polo shirt, untucked, with the collar up, plus a bandanna, and a Yankees hat to complement the blue jeans and special boots. While the MSNBC cameras looked on, Imus settled over the ball and teed off. He actually did well on his fairway work and was near the green in five, thanks to his ball striking a lady who had been watching from the cart path.

The putt for six had the distance but broke downhill left; seven was uphill and just off, leaving the tap-in for eight. On being interviewed immediately after the hole in a great MSNBC piece, Imus said, "If I hadn't have missed the last one, I would have had seven, right?" Mike Breen would later accuse him of an ugly ball-tampering incident by one of his associates that day in New Jersey that should have cost him a stroke. But Imus was sticking with eight and trying to plead that seven was what he deserved. No matter; the kids of the Tomorrow's Children's Fund welcomed the thirty-five thousand dollars.

The spread of the Internet has brought Imus fans together. There are more than a half-dozen Web sites dedicated to Imus. While all pay tribute in various ways, the fans from Bangor to D.C. to Tacoma can spend their time talking about Imus and his merry band of men over the keyboard now, and they can even do it in real time.

To go along with the Internet image of MSNBC, the cable network added a live Internet chat in real time with the *Imus in the Morning* program. Every morning from 6 to 9 A.M. eastern time, fans with names like JohnfrmDC, FirstRino, Marie, WVGal, and yes, even WichitaJim can be found talking about the happenings on the program and current events surrounding it. Some days it gets wild, with Democrats lining up on one side and Republicans on the other, firing off about President Clinton and Kenneth Starr. On other days, or even on the same day, a bunch of people make zucchini jokes.

The chat is overseen by several people from MSNBC. The hosts are Chas and Joe, who make sure the people and the language don't get too wild. They do a great job of keeping the chat moving, too. Chas keeps everyone feeling welcome, and

Joe contributes strange real-world news clips that always get the conversation stirred. If you attract their attention, mostly by making them laugh, you are usually assured of being immortalized on the imus.msnbc.com Web site under "The Good, the Bad and the Ugly" of the daily chat.

The strong competition is for the big payoff—making it on to the show. Every morning during the program the Imus control room at MSNBC's Secaucus, New Jersey, facility monitors the chat, looking for tasty comments and tidbits to actually put on the air. Jeremy Newberger and gang will flash a comment on as a graphic at the appropriate time, and if you are lucky, the ultimate payoff is that Imus will quote you.

If you are not an early-to-rise person, especially on the West Coast, where the chat runs from 3 to 6 A.M., there are several other choices. An Imus mailing list delivers discussion right to E-mail boxes, which lends itself to discussion of breaking news and Imus's reactions. The Internet news group, alt.fan.don-imus, is like a message board where people post all kinds of comments. A recent sampling of the group shows a war between Howard Stern and Imus fans, a discussion of Imus's appearance on Larry King, and whether King went easy on Imus, talk of how Imus's years of sobriety have given others the courage to get off drugs and alcohol.

The MS part of MSNBC provides what has to be the best Imus Web site on the Internet, and that's coming from someone who has an Imus Web site on the Internet. Jeremy Newberger, associate producer of Imus on MSNBC, is the individual primarily responsible for the Web site, found at imus.msnbc.com. On a regular basis, aside from the chat highlights, surfers get to participate in the program through a live chat, a bulletin board of fan postings, and live votes on topics of the day.

Imus.msnbc.com shines the brightest when Imus and the news converge, with links to important Web sites and interesting original content, like the first baby pictures of the newest Imus, Wyatt, and a picture of Don's old band days. They have embraced the ranch and have done a fantastic job of getting the word out and showing off the best stuff of the program that you could never get anywhere else. One thing you won't see on the imus.msnbc.com Web site, though, is a live feed of the show. Don't look for one in the near future, either. The two major obstacles are NBC and CBS. NBC wants to protect its affiliates' morning news and the *Today* program and may actually be happy to see MSNBC's cable penetration remain low. Another way for people to get something other than their channel wouldn't help (especially without commercials). Meanwhile, CBS, also eschewing the competition, prohibits its syndicated radio programs from being carried on the Internet.

# 14
## TWO GUYS AND MORE

In the spring of 1997, Villard published a book by a couple of brothers not known for their photography. In fact, Don Imus and Fred Imus are mostly known for talking on the radio and selling shirts, respectively. However, somewhere along the line someone discovered some of the fabulous photographs the brothers had taken in their spare time, as a hobby, and made them into a calendar for the Auto Body Express. Over the previous twenty years, Don and Fred had spent vacations looking at landscapes of the Southwest. Don had become a photo junkie in the early 1970s, starting out with a Polaroid and within weeks "owning every piece of equipment Nikon made." If you can make a calendar, why not a book, so *Two Guys, Four Corners and a Million Laughs* was born.

The book was a publishing success. Don and Fred plugged it considerably, selling over 130,000 copies in the span of a few months. It hit the *New York Times* and *Publishers Weekly* best-seller lists. The brothers even spent time on an East Coast publicity tour, autographing their book over thirty thousand times as they hit cities along the eastern seaboard. At the Boston book signing, in a bookstore just off Copley Place, the brothers had people waiting in line for over ninety minutes just to get two names scribbled in a book. The public-relations campaign was hot and heavy and even attracted the attention of the television media.

The now defunct *Spy* magazine, a New York–based glossy that poked fun at celebrities, used to have a section called "Logrolling in Our Time." In that section you would read how one writer would give stunning kudos to another and then receive a quid pro quo or some other benefit.

Now, we are not accusing CBS of logrolling. Right after *Two Guys, Four Corners* came out, another CBS newsmagazine, *48 Hours,* decided to profile "prickly personality" Don Imus. The same Don Imus heard on CBS Radio and who owned, according to him, "millions" of shares of CBS stock. The same Don Imus who frequently invited the anchor and managing editor of the *CBS Evening News,* Dan Rather, on his program.

So for the second time in fifteen months Imus was on CBS. Actually, three Imuses were on, as Don and Deirdre took Rather on a trip aboard *I-Force One* (Don's personal executive jet) to join Fred for a photo excursion in New Mexico—a look at the kinder, gentler side of America's first shock jock.

The piece ran alongside a story on the trial of Oklahoma City bomber Timothy McVeigh and a profile of some real life "twister" chasers. For the most part, it was an easygoing piece. It may have actually been pretty successful at showing the private Don Imus, as private as you can be in front of Dan Rather and a television crew. Rather good-naturedly asks Imus about some of the more controversial captions in the book while they await the perfect shot.

They get a nice photograph, but not before the trip takes a side turn, or more correctly, the plane does. It turned on to the hot tarmac in the middle of a New Mexico summer and proceeded to become mired in the black goo. A several-hundred-mile car trip rescued them and got them back to New York before Monday morning. (By the way, Rather and his crew reportedly reimbursed Imus for the equivalent plane fare for the trip so as not to be beholden to Don for the ride.)

MSNBC made the another connection for Imus, hooking Don and Fred up with Katie Couric on the *Today* show to talk about the book. It was tough to decide who would get a word in edgewise, but the chat stayed pleasant.

The success of *Two Guys, Four Corners* will live on in a sequel. Of course, the publisher is already calling Imus, trying to start work on it.

As the end of Imus's life grows closer than the beginning, he is starting to become more interested in his image and his legacy.

Even as this book is being written, Imus continues to show his interest in helping kids. His work on the WFAN radiothon broadcast for the Tomorrow's Children Fund and CJ Foundation for Kids has raised $13 million (as of February 1998) for the foundation. The donations helped establish the Imus/WFAN Center for Tomorrow's Children at Hackensack, N.J., Medical Center.

The work for kids took an interesting turn one day in March 1998 when Imus welcomed Paul Newman to the program. They glossed over the movie Newman was plugging and spent time talking about Newman's charities, like the Hole in the Wall Gang Camp in northwest Connecticut. Imus, newly inspired, spent his vacation week in New Mexico searching for a site where he could build the "Tomorrow-land Ranch."

Within a week after returning from New Mexico, Imus owned a chunk of land and was establishing the Imus Ranch Foundation. Seeding the ranch with $1 million of his own money, he set out to find donations to build a ranch where these "crippled kids" from the Tomorrow's Children's Fund could come and work the ranch. Of course, the *Imus* program being what it is, within days he was attacked by his on-air characters, and even Charles and Bernie, for developing a slave-labor camp, just to have someone to staff the ranch. Fans in MSNBC's Internet chat room even nicknamed the ranch "Rancho Bondage." On the air, Bernie once dubbed it "The Hole in the Lung Gang Camp" a great reference to Newman's current charity and Imus's past affliction.

All the talk of the ranch really helped show Imus's true power—the millions of listeners he has, unlike any book he might plug. Hamilton Jordan, a former Carter administration official, provided advice on how to set up the camp. Donations poured in from everywhere: roofing materials from Hartford, appliances from El Paso, computers from New York, and Longhorn cattle from Texas. A Texas oil man, whose ranch they considered but didn't end up buying, tossed in a bull. Tom Brokaw donated a horse from his ranch.

Don's paranoia over having to pay off the note to get the camp started soon began to fade as money and goods poured in. No one was ever really asked to help. The camp just seemed to take on momentum. When Imus spoke to his friend and New York Stock Exchange chairman and CEO Richard "Dick" Grasso about the project, Grasso told him raising $3.2 million to build it was "a slam dunk."

And it was, too, once he opened things up to his fans. Imus took the original 810 acres and parceled it out in one-acre blocks. Then he symbolically sold them. It took a little over a day before he was putting names on the waiting list for the chance to pay $5,000 for an acre that couldn't be built on. The first $4 million was in the bank, and the ranch had 810 "foremen."

The second sale was for the chance to work for the foremen as "wranglers." Two per acre, at a donation of $1,000 each, netted the ranch another $1.6 million. Building sponsorships went to corporations like American Express, Mentadent toothpaste, and even the New York Stock Exchange. At least two anonymous donations of $1 million were received by the ranch. Ted Turner even got involved, donating a dollar from every ticket sold for 1998's Goodwill Games. With a war chest of over $10 million, Don Imus was well on his way toward achieving his goal of having a free ranch for kids, one that they will *never* have to pay to visit.

The spread of the ranch grew, too. The original parcel of land was 810 acres, or about the size of Disney's Animal Kingdom theme park. Imus, in just a few months, continued to buy, purchasing a parcel of land here and leasing a parcel there. The Imus Ranch has since increased to over three thousand acres. The leased land would spark controversy, however. Not surprising, for Imus and controversy seem to go together.

Two New Mexico newspapers reported that, depending on whom you talk to, either a garbage dump or an old town was illegally cleared from land leased from the state that was to be taken over by the ranch. The area in dispute was possibly a historical site, creating one problem, and state workers were used to clear it, causing even more consternation. Even though Imus had not taken possession of the land when the work was done, he did agree to pay the state almost $6,700 for the work that had been done. Imus also offered an archaeological survey of the rest of the ranch to ensure that this problem did not repeat itself.

Imus has persisted in his dedication to making the Imus

# Imus Philanthropy

1983: $400,000 donation to families of those lost on Korean Airlines 007, shot down by a Soviet fighter plane

1990: WFAN Tomorrow's Children's Fund, CJ Foundation for SIDS radiothon begins. Proceeds would eventually turn into the Imus-WFAN Pediatric Center for Tomorrow's Children.

1991: appears with Susan St. James at sports benefit for Connecticut Special Olympics

1996: Imus's appearance in Bangor, Maine, benefits United Cerebral Palsy's Camp CaPella to the tune of $6,600.

1997: Imus shoots an eight at Fiddler's Elbow Country Club and successfully completes the "Teed Off" golf challenge, raising tens of thousands for the TCF.

1998: Imus donates the first $1 million to the Imus Ranch Foundation for purchase of 810 acres of land in Ribera, New Mexico, the future home of the Imus Ranch.

Ranch Foundation about the children. He pushed to keep costs down, not letting it be a foundation where more money was spent on administration than helping out those kids who come to visit. He also vowed that no child would ever pay to visit the ranch. He's arranged air transportation from the New York area; every child gets boots and jeans, like a real cowboy, and every kid is to be treated like one. While the ranch may be built with façades, like a saloon for the infirmary, it will be a working ranch, and the children will be expected to work. It's Don's own brand of therapy—treat them like kids, not like patients.

Don't think for a minute that life is easy being the I-Man heading into the twenty-first century, though. Don has had his share of problems in the late nineties. Lawsuits, death threats, and the media all weigh heavily on Don's shoulders.

He has had to deal with two major lawsuits. First, Judge Harold Rothwax sued Imus for libel after Don defended his wife on the air. Check out the chapter on Deirdre to get the whole story.

Imus was also sued by a woman working for the Chrysler Corporation. Marilyn Hobbs sent the I-Man a letter saying he had used the trademark "Jeep" incorrectly in his book *God's Other Son*. After feeling she was attacked on the air, she sued Imus and others for slander and libel, asking for $10 million.

A not-so-big fan in Connecticut wished a stalker with a deer rifle on the I-Man in retaliation for comments Don made on the air about President Clinton; a forty-three-year-old man allegedly sent some hateful E-mail to Don in early 1998 and was arrested. Imus beefed up his own personal security in light of the incident, most likely thanks to Bo Dietl's security company. The man's lawyer requested a psychological profile in the case, and the accused was put on two years' probation.

Land in Connecticut was also in the news. When Imus bought a new house on four acres in Westport (sticker price almost $6 million) and announced demolition plans, trouble brewed. Locals said structures on the property were historic and started a Stop Imus Committee. Imus threatened to tear everything down then and announced that if any newspaper printed a picture of his house, he would show pictures of the editors' houses on MSNBC.

The *Connecticut Post* uncovered what ended up being a tempest in a teapot when they found that Imus was delinquent in his tax payments and ran a front-page story. The error actually belonged to his bank, which was in charge of paying the taxes. Imus really won this battle, getting the *Post* to print not one but two retractions. Imus wanted the retraction to get front-page play, since the original story did, and the Bridgeport-based paper conceded. At last word, the I-Man had put his Southport house up for sale at an asking price of almost double what he paid for it. Maybe he is learning from Donald Trump.

So what is on the plate for Don Imus's future? Any chance of bringing back some of the classic characters? He has several projects in the pipeline right now that should be out shortly after this book is published, if not before.

To start off, the Imus brothers are committed to a sequel of their successful book *Two Guys, Four Corners.* As mentioned earlier in this chapter, Villard, their publisher, is already pushing for more photos. No title or publishing date has yet been set.

That will not be his only book, though. Don has signed a deal to be a contributor to a series of books with Random House. Called the Library of Contemporary Thought, the small books are published monthly. The first in the series was a John Feinstein book on Tiger Woods and a Vincent Bugliosi title on the *Jones vs. Clinton* case. No word yet on what Imus's ninety-six pages of thought will be, but you can be sure he will plug it when it comes out. No date set yet, either.

Imus has mentioned that he is working on a third book as well. Could we expect another novel from the I-Man? Well, since he seems to have covered Billy Sol Hargus well enough, don't expect a sequel there. We're hoping for something fictional, though. Some relaxed Imus reading is something to look forward to.

Then there was *Whittaker Chambers: A Biography,* the Sam Tanenhaus book that Imus went on and on about. After it failed to nail down any major book awards and after other continual frustrations with book awards, Don took matters into his own hands. He joined with Barnes & Noble to present the Imus American Book Awards. The Imus Awards will dish out a total of $250,000 in prizes to four books Imus and his panel of editors feel are deserving. They will not be selected, as he told *New York* magazine, by "a bunch of elitist precious yuppie shitheads."

A project that has been "on the books" for a while is the record album. After several 45s and albums, the last of which was published in 1974, Imus and his posse are headed back into the studio. Jim Steinman, who produced *Bat Out of Hell* for Meat Loaf, will produce. One of the hurdles that has been discussed is the use of music, since Rob's song parodies will play a big role and the karaoke tracks just won't cut it. My prediction: Imus won't stop plugging it when it comes out until he is on *Billboard*'s bestseller list.

Unfortunately, don't look forward to seeing Crazy Bob, Billy Sol Hargus, Moby Worm, or Geraldo Santana Banana on the album or even get revived on radio. All of those classic characters have been retired, gone with the memories of WNBC.

Don has worn many titles over his time: Shock Jock, Clinton basher, and even hate-radio star. I believe that when his contract ends somewhere after 2004, there will be plenty for us to look back on fondly and enjoy.

Of course, talking about the end of Don's career begs the question as to who, if anyone, would be his successor. It's easy to imagine in 2004, after thirty-six years in broadcasting, that Imus may want to hang up his microphone for good. Don will be sixty-four, almost mandatory retirement age in some companies. Here's some speculation as to what might happen:

**Charles McCord:** While he has shown no signs of slowing down, he has definitely done his time. With his wife, Connie, starting up a successful travel agency, there probably would not be an income issue. One guess is that Charles will be able to live comfortably and spend time with his show dogs and his fleet of cars. He could even keep his considerable talents sharp by writing books or even comedy. After Imus, there's no doubt

Charles will be able to call his own shots and be successful at whatever he chooses.

**Rob Bartlett:** He'd be in his mid-forties by then; if anyone in the crew might step in and take over the program, it would be Rob Bartlett. While his comedy has certainly had a political edge, I am not sure he's had the day-to-day on-air experience to just step into the job. That's assuming he'd want to. His stand-up is sharp, and he will have put in close to twenty years with Imus by then. It's a toss-up. He may want the steady work of a daily show and going home to his kids. He may want to get out while the getting is good and move on to something new.

**Larry Kenney:** As with Charles, by the time Imus retires, Larry Kenney will have had a full career. If he decides to take over, one thing Kenney has going for him is radio experience. Unlike Bartlett, Kenney has spent a ton of time behind the microphone spinning records. Would he want to get full time behind the mike again? Doubtful; the man at this point is making good money doing his voice-over work for commercials and could definitely make a good living at doing just that. Plus, there are easier things to do than get up at four in the morning to be on radio. With all his contacts, Larry could easily make a few calls and end up on a quiet shift at WCBS-FM, if he desired.

**Bernard McGuirk:** As the youngest of the candidates, we don't see Bernie just stepping into Imus's shoes. While he does have moments of occasional hilarity, his time behind the glass has not prepared him to take over on 100 radio stations across the country. His comedy is not consistent, and right now he has positioned himself as being too right wing to just fall into Imus's seat as a major media mogul. Now, this doesn't mean that McGuirk could not make it on radio, it just means he may want to consider places like Palmdale and Sacramento.

**Don Imus:** Deirdre, Don, and Wyatt will head off to the ranch. In addition to the philanthropic aspect of the ranch, Don is probably designing the ranch to be self-sustaining, which would allow him to live comfortably. Of course, with the millions he is making annually on his current contract, he had better have

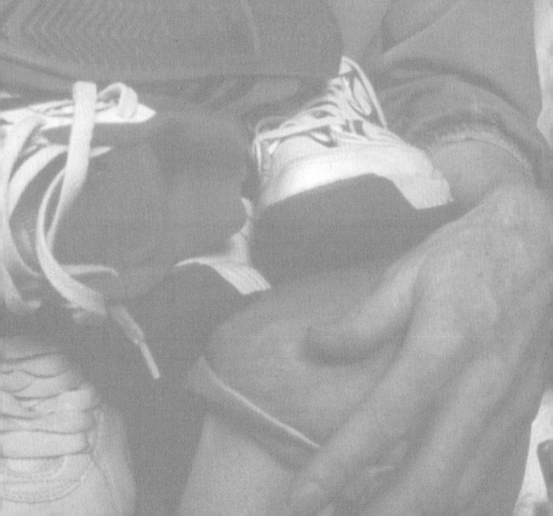

## Major Awards Won

1. 1969: Medium Market Disc Jockey of the Year
2. 1970: Major Market Disk Jockey of the Year
3. 1971: Major Market Personality of the Year
4. 1991: Major Market Personality of the Year
5. 1995: Syndicated Personality of the Year
6. 1996: Broadcasting Hall of Fame, 1996
7. 1997: *Time* magazine's 25 Most Influential Americans

a few dollars left over. Plus, I think he likes the idea of raising his son the way he was raised, on a ranch in the Southwest.

The most likely scenario is that someone would not "replace" him at all; instead, they would just fill his time slot. When *Seinfeld* ended, no one replaced Jerry.

In New York, WFAN could easily slide *Mike and the Mad Dog* to mornings and let the sports-crazed fans tear up the phone lines, or maybe it could be split into two shows? One might stay on mornings; the other, afternoons. Nationally, CBS Radio will try to keep the business by spreading it out to its different holdings. Howard Stern would probably get some stations; they might even make an aggressive push to move Washington, D.C.'s Don and Mike to mornings and sell the slightly tamer version of Stern.

In February 1996, Richard Turner wrote a thoughtful article about Imus and his political guests. Turner basically accused Imus of being part of a game that cares more about celebrity than issues:

> (Imus) doesn't worry how he's playing, and this is his appeal. Every interviewer has an angle—trying to look smart, make a point, get ratings, win fans, enhance fees on the lecture circuit. Imus is too burned out to care about any of this, and his listeners understand this. They don't worship him. They don't like the country music he plays. They wouldn't even necessarily take his advice seriously about whom to vote for. But they know who he really is, and he's something like them.

# PART III

# IMUS'S POSSE

# 15
## IGNORE THE MAN BEHIND THE CURTAIN — CHARLES MCCORD

The story of *The Wizard of Oz* is familiar to people young and old. A man from Missouri, hidden behind a curtain and speaking through a character, helps a band of unlikely pals complete their mission. You can draw this same comparison between Don Imus and Charles Everett McCord. Imus is the loud front and the man with the mission; the man pulling a lot of strings behind the scenes is Springfield, Missouri, native Charles McCord.

McCord's birth date has not been determined, but a rough guess puts it at 1941. McCord grew up in Springfield and ended up with some rather famous schoolmates. Former Missouri governor and now senator John Ashcroft was a member of the same class as Chuck. Another schoolmate made his way to radio, too, talk-show host Jim Bohannon. Probably the most important classmate was a lady by the name of Connie. She and Charles were high school sweethearts and have ended up being married for thirty-five years and counting.

McCord, like Imus, also spent some time in the military. Mr. McCord was in the army. Imus says he was a nurse. Nevertheless McCord served his country. When his army tour was over in 1963, he went home to Springfield and headed for the local pool hall. His father got Chuck out of the eight-ball game by talking a friend into giving him a job at KICK. Chuck was assigned the job of writing ads. McCord had barely been there a week when shots rang out in Dallas and bells rang on the wire machine in the newsroom. McCord was the first in the station to find out Kennedy had been shot. Just a few days later, McCord would get his first on-air assignment, albeit a sad one. He broke into news announcing by reading Cardinal Cushing's eulogy of slain president John F. Kennedy.

McCord's climb up the radio ladder may have been even more impressive than the rise of Imus, Stern, or any of his cohorts. After moving across town to another Springfield station, he made the jump to one of the premier radio stations in the nation, WFAA in Dallas. In a twist of fate, he worked in the same plaza where those shots had been fired just a few years earlier.

One of McCord's next stops as a radio gypsy was Washington, D.C.'s WTOP. The station was preparing to go all news, and Charles McCord would be joining an impressive group of radio journalists. The man who would go on to be Diane Sawyer's coanchor on *Primetime Live*, Sam Donaldson, worked with McCord, as did the woman who would coanchor with Dan Rather, Connie Chung. Bill Lynch and Gary Nunn, both longtime CBS newsmen, were also members of the WTOP team. McCord even got to work with a man he would bump into again in New York, Warner Wolf.

He worked his way up and ended up in the Emerald City, at WNBC in the early 1970s, not long after Don Imus arrived. The two were teamed together on and off, since there was a rotating group of newsmen in the morning, but McCord and Imus soon became fast friends. Imus, naturally, was the front man for the show; and McCord, the straight man while doing the news twice an hour.

It was behind the scenes where McCord would bring the Imus show to life. Even McCord can't pinpoint the exact time he started being a "writer" for the I-Man. He told *RTNDA Communicator,* a broadcast news trade magazine, that he just did some funny traffic reports at first, before he and Imus became a full-fledged team. It must not have taken too long, because Imus's *This Honky's Nuts* album credits Charles as a cowriter on most of the LP.

Just because Imus was in exile in Cleveland didn't mean McCord was out of work. He spent time working for Jack Thayer, who was supervising NBC's all-news radio network. You may remember Thayer as the man who hired Imus in Sacramento and later brought him to Cleveland. Thayer's news network was a million-dollar bust.

McCord was actually the first guy Imus called when Don found out he was coming back from Cleveland. McCord launched into something creative. When "God's Chosen, Re-Rosen Disc Jockey" took back the WNBC's air chair in September 1979, the voice may have been Don's, but the words were McCord's. After each day's show, McCord began writing taped segments for Imus's cast of characters, like the Right Reverend Dr. Billy Sol Hargus, the Baptist preacher; Crazy Bob, the twisted storyteller; and Geraldo Santana Banana, the vice president and general manager of *Imus in the Morning*. He even helped create Moby Worm.

A few little-known facts you may not have noticed. McCord's place on the show is at the *right* hand of the I-Man in the studio, which just goes to show you he's Don's right-hand man. McCord has been given a grammar award for his corrections of the I-Man. What about the frequently used electrocution sound effect of a man screaming from the shock of Old Sparky? The voice writhing in pain is none other than McCord's. Moreover, despite Larry King's comments while interviewing Imus in July 1998, Charles is not coming out with a book anytime soon, though he does get acknowledged in *God's Other Son* for doing a wood chopping job worthy of Paul Bunyan.

McCord had some extracurricular activities, too. While Larry and Rob have made some extra dough with their voices, McCord was also able to put his to work in the field of sports. I don't know why the job lasted only one season, but for one shining year he was the voice of NFL on NBC. McCord was the guy who said, "The NFL on NBC is brought to you by . . ." and then listed off the name of some motor oil, a delivery service, and a beer. It might not be as exciting as being a cartoon voice, but it's easy work.

He may have needed the money to pay for his summer home. Or he may have used the money to buy it. McCord's Arkansas vacation home even caught the attention of President Clinton during one of Imus's chats with the leader. (McCord didn't buy a home in the Whitewater development; he's got a quiet little place on a lake in northeastern Arkansas.)

Charles and his wife, Connie, live on what could easily be called an estate. The couple have lived in Wayne, New Jersey, for years, raising their son, Les. Not without some controversy, though. In 1990, when the Patterson diocese planned to close the prep school Les was attending, the McCords sued to keep the school open.

McCord is a deeply religious man and teaches Bible study in his home. Of course, since he only taught classes in the fall and winter, he had to hear Imus hammer him for not loving little baby Jesus during the summer.

What does McCord do to stay sane after working with Imus every day? He has had lots of hobbies. He once held his private pilot's license. At one time, he owned a Corvette, and still might. The time during which he bought the car is still referred to by Imus as Chuck's male menopause period. Lately, he and Connie have taken to showing dogs.

Actually make that *dog,* singular. Ozzie is his name. A cute little Boston terrier McCord keeps boarded in Maryland or Pennsylvania. The McCords will occasionally take a weekend road trip to visit their dog. (Somewhere along the line they also make visits to their son in college.) Ozzie, named after the Gold Glove–winning shortstop of the St. Louis Cardinals, Ozzie Smith, made his debut at the Westminster Kennel Club show in early 1998. Actually, Ozzie does have one of those long-ass fu-fu dog names, but we'll stick with Ozzie.

In that one appearance, Ozzie may have gotten more media attention than Rin Tin Tin in his day. Imus encouraged McCord before the dog show started, and it was obvious that Don wanted the pooch to win best of show. The normal media coverage of the USA Network broadcast shined down on Ozzie as well as the MSNBC crew documenting the dog's life that day. The *New York Daily News* even wrapped a story around the twelve-pound terrier. Ozzie was not up to the task, however. He did not even win best of breed, much less make it to the finals. Expect Ozzie to make a comeback, though; he was only two at the time, and his father was a champion.

Connie McCord, also known as "Frog" by Imus, spends her time running her own business, Tips on Trips Travel, a New Jersey–based full-service travel agency that actually uses a famous newscaster on its voice mail. Rumor has it that if you can find the location, you can probably find McCord helping out in the back room when he is not on the air.

Speaking of voice mail and answering machines, don't expect to call the McCord household and get through. All the callers are met with a succinct message voiced by Charles McCord that all calls are screened.

Instead of keeping up with the Joneses, the McCords have had to keep up with Imus to a certain extent. McCord bought Don's old Rolls-Royce, and he also owns a Jeep. Since Don would call him and want to talk about the television programs he was watching, Don had a DSS satellite system put into the McCord house.

# 16

## MRS. IMUS AND BABY MAKES SEVEN?

The first meeting between Deirdre Coleman and Don Imus is a mystery. Read *People Weekly* and it will tell you that the two met in November 1992, when Deirdre was a ring-card girl for a charity boxing match. A different article speculates that they met when Imus sat on the bench for a Fordham basketball game and she was a cheerleader. A third has her auditioning for a role as a voice on the *Imus in the Morning* program. One way or another, the former cheerleader met the aging radio personality, and they began dating.

The two were definitely an item. They attended a correspondents' dinner in Washington and posed for pictures in *Esquire,* Imus standing tall in cowboy garb, Deirdre sitting beside him, clutching his leg. The pair must have hit it off famously, because according to all accounts, just over two years later they tied the knot.

He was fifty-four at the time, according to *People Weekly,* and she was twenty-nine. When you do the math, that is a twenty-five-year age difference. That had to have created some family friction among his daughters, considering his youngest, Ashleigh, was twenty-six or twenty-seven at the time, two years younger than her new stepmother.

However, Don put aside the age issue, according to *People.* "There was a question of whether I should adopt her or marry her. She's already practicing wiping oatmeal from off my chin. I wasn't running around looking for a younger woman, but I fell in love with her. She's interesting, funny, and smart. What was I supposed to do?"

The pair were married on a Navajo Indian reservation

near the four corners of New Mexico, on December 29, 1994. One has to wonder: After all the harassing he gives to callers and guests who sleep together before they are married, did Imus sample the milk before he bought the cow? Either way, it's not as if Deirdre were a presidential intern. They can do whatever they like behind closed doors.

Behind closed doors is where they like to spend their time, too. Their home life revolves around a two-story penthouse on Central Park West. Imus has alluded to the fact that he can see the great lawn of Central Park from his residence. Inside, it's just the family and the overly pampered cat. Collins, named after a former coworker, Jim Collins, is a Himalayan blue point. As much as Imus likes to give McCord a hard time about Ozzie, it's doubtful that Ozzie gets limo rides to the vet, as does Collins.

The Imus family will rarely be seen out at a New York nightspot or big Broadway opening. Those things just don't interest Imus, and running into fans just does not give him any pleasure. Of course, that doesn't stop his wife from trying to coax him out to places. Once, at a play, Deirdre would have to repeat everything for the hard-of-hearing I-Man, causing everyone else in the audience to laugh. Then, a few moments later, Don's characteristic cackle could be heard.

They travel privately, too. Imus owns one-sixteenth of a plane and uses it for his vacation getaways. One could speculate that he may have the private jet because he may not be welcome on any of the major carriers after a blowout with American Airlines. The truth is, though, it is more a matter of convenience. It's easier for Imus to travel to small cities like Bangor this way, and he does like to stay away from the crowds. He can also get on the plane with his gun, no questions asked.

Deirdre became a frequent contributor and a welcome caller to the show. She would give the fans deep insights to the real Imus at home. She tells that upon moving in, there were nothing but paths between the books to the couch and the desk. One of her stories alleges he was shouting at her because she couldn't untangle the Christmas lights. Neither one of them could get the vacuum cleaner to work. Mike Breen even attacked the I-Man on the air for his sickening little smoochie conversations with his wife on the phone.

Deirdre's mission, aside from spending her time waiting for the opportunity to wipe oatmeal from Don's chin, is to pursue a career in acting. In the fall of 1997 one of the season's first episodes of the USA Network program *Silk Stalkings* featured Deirdre Coleman-Imus. Mrs. Imus played the role of a conniving stepdaughter who kills off her stepmother's pets. The program ends with a bizarre chase scene. Deirdre runs into a field set up for horse training, and you actually see her hurdle the horse jumps. She is finally caught facedown in a horse pie. Overall, it was a very stiff performance by Deirdre, who seemed to be shouting all her lines.

Her other acting experience was a little more upstanding. In Bo Dietl's movie *One Tough Cop,* she plays a New York City emergency-services worker who helps the star, Stephen Baldwin, save a young child.

Imus is a man who will defend his wife until the bitter end, lawsuits and all. In September 1997, Deirdre was called to be a juror in a Manhattan court and was assigned to the court of Judge Harold Rothwax. Imus, thinking it would be fun, paid one of his reporter friends to cover the trial. This ended up making Deirdre so uncomfortable that she asked to speak to the judge in private. Rothwax ended up publicly speaking to Ms. Coleman-Imus, and after asking to be excused because of the attention her husband was putting on things, she received a public dressing-down. Imus had a fit on the air, calling him Judge Scuzzwax, among other things. Imus called the judge on the carpet for the poor treatment of his wife, who did end up being excused from the jury.

The judge, probably knowing a few good lawyers, decided to take on the I-Man. Rothwax's reputation was one of being a litigious judge. When Rothwax fell near a park construction area earlier that year, he brought suit against the construction company. A suit was brought against John Donald Imus for slander. Imus contended that Rothwax was a public figure, making the burden of proof for slander much higher. If Rothwax thought those comments were bad, Imus turned up the heat. He sent out his intrepid reporter, Bernard McGuirk, to check up on the construction accident. Bernie put a chalk outline of where Rothwax fell and made sure to point out the line from the local liquor store to the spot that the judge tripped.

Imus offered to settle out of court several times, with a proposal to make a large donation to one of Rothwax's favorite charities. The untimely death of Harold Rothwax from a heart attack ended the lawsuit, though Imus still offered the donation.

Just a few weeks after Deirdre was excused from jury duty, Imus got the call to be a juror. He left early and spent parts of two days at the courthouse, waiting to get picked. His secrets of getting out of jury duty: Never hear a case against a sponsor or potential sponsor and advocate the death penalty in all cases, even one as mild as jaywalking.

Imus may have been excused from jury duty, but he got in hot water with his wife. Deirdre makes every effort to take care of her husband by keeping him on a vegetarian diet consisting of bean sprouts and tofu. While doing a story on citizen Imus going to court, the *New York Daily News* captured Imus buying hot dogs from a pushcart vendor on camera.

Not long after the court stuff, Deirdre became pregnant. The fans would not find out as early as the I-Man, though. If you were keen enough to catch them, there were plenty of hints dropped along the way. Like a politician, Imus kept talking around the point, but he never hit the mark. For example, he was caught by MSNBC during a radio break talking to Mike Breen about the baby. Breen kidded him about being more excited about the baby than his ratings. On another occasion, he was yelled at by friend Bernadette Castro for talking trash when he was about to be a father again. He simply stared at her and said, "What are you, nuts?" Even *New York Post* columnist Liz Smith seemed to have the inside scoop before the listeners, announcing in February that Deirdre was "expecting."

It drove the fans nuts. People on the Internet chat, the news group, and the mailing list were speculating about everything regarding the baby. The name was debated. Would the child be named after Fred, since Fred named his son after Don? Would it be named after Whittaker Chambers, since Don had been so obsessed with him? When was it due? June, September, October? I even ran a poll on the Web site: "Do you think Deirdre Coleman-Imus is pregnant?" It didn't matter that

the hints had been dropped; 25 percent of those voting still said
no. Imus fan Chris Ramsey, owner of an Arkansas nursery
called Ramsey Nursery, jumped the gun and on first speculation sent Don and Deirdre a Grow Baby jumper.

On April 6, 1998, he officially broke the silence. At a little
after nine eastern time, he told the world that Deirdre was due
to give birth to their first child. Frederic Wyatt was due in a
couple of months. He would be Don's fifth child and his first
boy.

Thanks to MSNBC's daily-electronic-mail Imus newsletter,
here's how the announcement sounded that morning. Imus
casually dropped it in while he was talking about the ranch:

> DON IMUS: . . . and etched into the stone is the name
> "William Imus 1884" and I got to thinking about that
> in the past few days and I thought, man, what a great
> idea that would be. To take just regular people's
> names and to do that. So that, long after I'm gone and
> Deirdre and this kid we're having . . . Did I tell you
> about that?
>
> CHARLES MCCORD: What?
>
> DON IMUS: That my wife is pregnant? I didn't tell you?
>
> CHARLES MCCORD: No.
>
> BERNARD MCGUIRK: Get outta town.
>
> DON IMUS: So we're having a little boy in two months.
> Who I've already named Frederic Wyatt and we're
> going to drag this little dummy out there and make
> him work on the ranch. And it's a great way to grow
> up. And hopefully he'll want to do this when they
> have to wheel me out on the front porch there and
> mush is dribbling out of my (mumble mutter
> mutter).

Once the ice was broken, you would have thought Don
had never been a father before, even with four daughters. Of
course, between getting caught up in the success of his radio
show and his extensive alcohol and drug abuse, it's doubtful
that there was a lot of time for the girls. On the air now, he
talked about how fat Deirdre was getting, how difficult it was to
put together a car seat, and how little he wanted to make his

den baby-safe. After all, this was a man who lived alone for fifteen years, and within the space of the next five, he would
have a new wife and a bouncing baby boy around the house.

All of the talk and speculation came to an end when a
healthy Fredric Wyatt Imus was born on July 3, 1998, at 11:39
A.M., weighed seven pounds and eleven ounces, and arrived
only two days late. Don was on vacation that week but was
already antsy about the birth.

Now, as Wyatt grows up, so do the stories. Once the first
month had passed, Imus was talking about the little guy every
day. He would complain about Wyatt's sleeping habits or something minor, but, surprisingly, he never went into full rant
about dirty diapers, even though he claimed that they were
going to go all natural and use cloth diapers. Imus plans on
having Wyatt ride before he can walk, which probably terrifies
his mom.

What about Wyatt's sisters? Where are they now? Imus has
said on the air that his relationship has been strained with all of
them at times, possibly because he has remarried such a young
woman, though two daughters did attend Dad's second wedding.
Another reason for the strain may be the fact that Imus has said
he cut them off financially when they turned thirty.

Of all the girls, he seems to talk about Ashleigh the most.
The youngest, she is an NYU graduate who went into teaching
and now is living in the South. Another, Nadine, at one time
was an editor for *Mademoiselle,* the fashion magazine. Where
Toni and Elizabeth and even Harriet are, no one knows. It may
be that they want to protect their privacy.

Imus, speaking with Al Roker once, said he thought it was okay
to have two wives. You should be allowed to make one mistake
and go on. Don and Deirdre both seem as happy as can be.
They have good reason to be; they will soon have four houses:
the two in Connecticut, the Central Park penthouse, and the
ranch. Plenty of places for Imus to watch television, Deirdre
to read, and Wyatt to play.

Will there be a sixth Imus child? Don says one is enough
for now. Once he gets baby Wyatt up in that saddle at the ranch
and sees all the fun he is having, you can bet he'll be reaching
for the Viagra again.

# 17

## BROTHER FRED

red and Don Imus are like the proverbial "two peas in a
pod." A very strange pod to be sure but a pod nonetheless.
The pair grew up together on the ranch and have stuck
together all their lives. In fact, Don considers Fred one of his
best friends, next only to Deirdre. It would be hard from looking at them to tell that Fred is actually two years younger than
Don. If Don looks like Jack Palance, then Fred looks like Gabby
Hayes. Just because they are two peas in a pod doesn't mean
that Fred doesn't possess a flair of his own; witness some of
the things he does.

After growing up on the Arizona and California ranches,
Fred watched his brother head off to the U.S. Marine Corps. As
soon as he could, he joined up, and there was no playing in
the band for Fred; he did his brother one better. Fred joined
the U.S. Army, and was assigned to the 101ˢᵗ Airborne Division.
During his service, aside from the excitement inherent in
jumping from planes, Fred had the good fortune of serving and
jumping with one of America's more famous soldiers, William
Westmoreland.

Fred later produced Don's program in Cleveland for a
while, and Don desperately tried to get Fred his own radio
show as early as the 1970s. Fred was also on several radio stations and was working as a country disc jockey as late as 1983
in El Paso.

Fred did seem to have a better flare for the music industry, though. While Don had done the singing and Fred was
writing in the early years, it was Fred who had the hit. His
song *"I Don't Want to Have to Marry You,"* sung by Jim Ed

Brown and Helen Cornelius, hit the top of the charts and actually won Fred an award.

No matter what his job, Fred always had a love of classic cars. It inspired him to open his own auto-body shop in El Paso; moreover, he was looking for work after the radio station he was working at closed. Fred would fix up classic cars, like 1957 Chevys, and sell some paint in a shop off the interstate. It was his brother's idea that would make him the head of a clothing and merchandising empire.

Fred started the Auto Body Express (ABX) in El Paso, with a simple mention from Don about selling a few shirts out of his body shop. Imus fans went nuts for them, and the phone began ringing off the hook, with people looking for denim workshirts instead of cherry-red metallic for their Chevy trucks. Since the shop was right off I-10, people would even stop by for their fix of Fred's goodies.

The next thing you know, the ABX was a million-dollars-plus-a-year business, attracting the attention of magazines like *Texas Monthly*. With people stopping by and orders continuing to increase, it was time for a change. The auto body shop closed, and the clothing business was set up in Santa Fe, New Mexico.

The ABX has everything Imus; from hats with four-legged Fred on them (that's a dog) to denim work shirts, belts, even bathrobes. Most of the items come embroidered with a logo that features a turquoise buffalo in front of a cactus and a red and gold setting sun. One of the great features of this logo is that it's subtle. The turquoise buffalo is something a fellow Imus fan would recognize immediately, but you don't get a bunch of Stern fans screaming "baba booey" at you. We may as well give Fred a giant plug: ABX merchandise is available at two stores, the main location in Santa Fe and the store at Mohegan Sun Casino in Connecticut. You can also buy Fred's stuff by mail order from a glossy catalog or on the Internet at www.autobodyexpress.com.

As the ABX has grown, Fred has branched out into new items. Turquoise Buffalo Tortilla Chips and his Hot Stuff salsa have blanketed the land. It seems that in just about every town there is an Imus radio show, you will find someplace selling Fred's chips and salsa. The chips are not turquoise-colored; they are delicious corn chips made by the Cape Cod Potato Chip Company. The back of the package will tell you that their size is three times that of the guitar picks he used while writing his hit song. If you have a jar of the salsa on a shelf in your house, you may have a collector's item and not know it. The name changed in 1997, and they got rid of the paper tops in 1998, so hide it away and you may make a few bucks on it.

Fred is serious about his salsa, too. He insists on all-natural ingredients, much to the disappointment of his manufacturer and his brother (read business partner) and accountants as well, because this drives up the salsa's price. Fred believes his formula is the best, though. He has even showcased his product at the grocery trade conventions. He started off by supplying little stores that requested it—places like Mel's Diesel in Lincoln, Nebraska, and Chris Ramsey's Ramsey Nursery in Harrison, Arkansas. Ramsey Nursery was the first chips-and-salsa remote location, after Ramsey, an acquaintance of Charles McCord's, called Fred and ordered a few cases. Chris says that Arkansas governor Huckabee is a frequent salsa-and-chips customer. The requests continued to grow, and now Fred's Southwest Salsa is fighting it out with products like Tostitas for space on the store shelves. He's also made some headway on the East Coast, with stores like Edwards, Waldbaums, and Stop and Shop.

There have been days when Fred might wish he was back in El Paso. He has had to spend some considerable time getting his foot out of his mouth after comments on the radio stirred the pot of controversy. A prime example is that of the "Mayoral Saga."

In mid-1997, after Don attacked the mayor of Santa Fe, calling her "a slug who is antiwhite and antitourist," the brothers decided that Fred was going to run for mayor of that city. Republican strategist Mary Matalin was even recruited to consult on Fred's campaign. The big problem was that Fred didn't actually live in the Santa Fe city limits, making him ineligible for a mayoral run.

Fred was back in the news after he attacked Mexican Americans during a conversation with Don. He lashed out at some people in Hernandez and in general said they were more concerned about drinking than reading and that he wouldn't hire any Mexicans to work at the Auto Body Express. Protesters lined up outside the ABX, asking people to boycott the store and banish Imus from New Mexico. His hiring practices were scrutinized after several Mexican workers had left the ABX, but he was cleared. In the end, Fred did end up apologizing.

Not all of Fred's troubles have engendered controversy, though. In a moment that was classic Fred, he presented his brother with a problem one morning while they were speaking on the radio. It seems Fred had lost a cantaloupe. Somewhere in Fred's place was a ripe, fresh melon, and it was missing. Things do get misplaced, but something the size of a melon? It boggles the mind.

We will not leave you with the impression that Fred is some dunce, dependent on his brother for support. Fred is a successful businessman and does well, famous brother or not. Fred's dunce character, much like Bernard's racist character, just happens to complement the radio program.

Fred does have an official job on the *Imus in the Morning* program. He is the official prognosticator, broadcasting his "Jeep Eagle Sports Lock of the Week." Fred will pick football games when they are in season and NASCAR races most of the rest of the time unless something big like the Final Four or World Series is going on. How much of a lock is Fred's Sports Lock? Aside from some spectacular upsets, you can probably do as well picking against him as with him.

Fred has had a lot of fun with the MSNBC broadcast. Early on, using the convergence of the Internet and television, they set up a small camera in Fred's place so that we could watch Fred when he chatted with Don. The pictures were jumpy, but the moments were classic. One morning, Fred came on as Santa Claus, with his little red hat on, and said, "Ho ho ho, Santa needs a ho." Another morning he appeared with an inflatable rubber doll, the kind that desperate men turn to for companionship. It seemed to catch on with the viewers, though. During Don's appearance in Sioux City, Iowa, he was given a gift for Fred: an inflatable rubber sheep.

Fred has become famous enough to meet another renowned American general. Instead of jumping out of a plane with him like Westmoreland, former general Norman Schwartzkof came to Fred's office in Santa Fe to interview Fred for *NBC Nightly News* in October 1996. The general talked to Fred about his views, which included the latter's very quotable quote "You can never have too many guns or too many trucks." The morning after it aired, Don was wise enough to dissect the piece on his radio show, trashing Fred's views about guns and life.

If you want to know more about Fred, you can read his book. Yes, first music and radio and then a book about the salsa man. *The Fred Book* is short, both in number of pages (114) and size (maybe five by seven). Coauthored by Mike Lupica and with an introduction by Don, the book contains various opinions of Fred's on life, liberty, and the pursuit of women. The differences between this book and several others Don has discussed on the program are notable. First, he didn't plug it mercilessly, and second, it never made any bestseller list. That may be because you could have read most of it while standing in the aisle at the book store and not have been disturbed by the clerk. Did we mention that the book was short?

Fred also seems to have a love-hate relationship with Laura Ingraham. The conservative columnist is a frequent guest on Don's show, often inviting comments from Fred like "she buys her clothes at a garage sale." Fred seems to have a soft spot for Laura, though. The inflatable doll was a blonde, and he named one of the animals at the ranch after her. Unlike Laura the cow, the human Ms. Ingraham cannot stick her own tongue up her nose.

Fred does have a love life, Ms. Ingraham not withstanding. He often speaks about his ex-wife, Phyllis, and their present hate-hate relationship. Fred seems to have a better relationship with Phyllis's parents and will occasionally visit his ex-in-laws. Of course, they are the grandparents of his four children. The youngest of the three is still with Mom; the oldest works for

American Airlines. You have probably heard talk of Donny, named after Fred's brother, who still lives with Fred in Santa Fe. Donny has been picked to be the technical guru at the ranch's Art Barn. That means he will be responsible for the cameras and stuff for the broadcast, which also means he will probably get yelled at by his uncle.

Today, at least, it looks as if Fred will be spending more of his future time in Ribera, New Mexico, instead of Santa Fe. Ribera is home to the Imus Ranch, and Fred has been an important part of it. He helped his brother select the land and has been the foreman for the ranch's construction.

Fred has been taking care of the livestock that will call the ranch home for quite some time. The animals on the ranch will be very diverse. In addition to the longhorn named after Ms. Ingraham, there is a longhorn bull named Tim Russert II. Tim I died in July 1998, possibly of eating too much alfalfa. Fred has human names for his other animals-pets, too. Four-Legged Fred is a dog that even has his own ABX hat! There is a horse named Phyllis and one named Larry (after Larry Kenney). Donkeys and sheep will also live on the over three thousand acres in Ribera.

Fred might seem a little quirky on the radio, but he most likely feels at home on the ranch. One thing is for sure: Fred is no Imus junior. He is a true Southwest original.

# 18
#####
# BOWLING FOR VOICES —
# LARRY KENNEY

If you had to pick which member of Imus's radio team had the most broadcasting experience, whom would you choose? Well, Bernie, Lou, Rob, and Breen are out—too young. Don started in 1968, but Charles topped that when he read Cardinal Cushing's eulogy for Kennedy in November 1963. Larry Kenney takes the gold, getting his start just a few months before McCord, in August 1963.

As his bio reads, "It all started at a little 5,000-watt radio station in Peoria, Illinois." Larry was just fifteen years old when he started spinning hot wax as a local disc jockey. He would find that a career in broadcasting would "provide a moderate income, yet require no heavy lifting," so he packed his bags and began the strange road trip that is life in broadcasting.

We mentioned earlier that Cleveland appeared to be a "disc-jockey incubator." Larry Kenney passed through the radio hothouse as well, spending time at WKYC. His resumé lists other prestigious stations, too. Larry also worked at the famous WOWO in Fort Wayne, Indiana, prior to Cleveland, and Chicago's WJJD.

It was in Chicago where he started working with Imus. Kenney used his voice to his advantage and worked with Imus beginning in 1973, calling in as "Richard Nixon" to name one. Kenney would also contribute to Don's "Imus in the Evening" nightclub act.

It was 1974 when Kenney would finally move to the city that never sleeps. What is more interesting, though, is that his job would have him *competing* against Imus. Kenney would host the morning show at 1050 WHN, the same station that, through the strange vicissitudes of broadcasting, he would return to over twenty years later, as a contract player for 66 WFAN. Imus and Kenney would both host their individual shows in the morning. Kenney would then make his way over to 30 Rock to record some voices.

One morning, Imus was still on the air when Kenney walked into the studio. Of course, Imus couldn't just compliment Kenney right off; he first apologized to him for beating him in the ratings. Then Don would graciously go on to say what a great job Kenney had done on a commercial for Twizzlers and even gave it what must have been a free play so everyone could listen.

Kenney spent most of his time in New York playing country music and must have been pretty good at it. *Billboard* magazine named him America's Best Country Music Disc Jockey in 1976 and again in 1978.

By 1980, Larry had left WHN and was on the NBC payroll full-time. The station that just five years before had carried the *Imus in the Morning* program on the FM dial, WNBC-FM, was now WYNY-FM. Larry Kenney was the host of the morning show, broadcast out of a studio just down the hall from the I-Man.

An article in the *New York Times*, written by Anna Quindlen, tells about Kenney with a special guest, Mayor Ed Koch. The mayor was not on to discuss the issues but as guest deejay for an hour. Koch spun some Paul Simon and Anne Murray records and joked around during his hour behind the turntables. Before turning the job back over to Kenney, he left him with a warning: "After my three terms, maybe I'll come back as a disk jockey."

For Larry Kenney, though, it wasn't all about playing hit records. He would definitely keep his voice busy and try his hand at some other very diverse jobs. One of the early ones, aside from Imus voices, was in 1976. Up to this point, and ever since, he has been mostly camera shy. But from 1976 to 1979 he was the host of a game show. No, Kenney wasn't kissing up on *Family Feud* or trying to get people to the top of the *$25,000 Pyramid*. It was bowling for cash that drew Mr. Kenney to television. For three years, he was the host of WOR-TV's *Bowling for*

*Dollars*. Every night, bowling ball–laden men and women would attempt strikes and spares, looking for Mr. Kenney to give them the big payoff.

Even before the voice man ventured into television, he was making money from his impersonations. In 1974, Larry recorded "The Honest to God, We Really Mean It, Very Last Nixon Album." Larry "Road Hog" Kenney, as Don would later call him, joined with the Imus brothers on records as well. Imus and Kenney would take some Fred Imus–written tunes and attempt to sing them. However, all details of the enterprise seem to have been burned or shredded.

It is his voices that he is known the most for, and that may have made Larry Kenney even more successful than anything he has done on radio. He turned to the lucrative world of voice-overs for commercials. How well does this pay? Well, for the average voice-over person out there, $250 for thirty *seconds'* worth of work is probably on the low side. Larry Kenney is in much more demand.

It's likely that Kenney is now in his second generation of enticing children to eat sugary cereals. Since the 1970s, every time a kid parroted the ads, with Sonny saying, "I'm coo-coo for Cocoa Puffs," he was copying Larry Kenney. Every time a kid screams, "I want Count Chocula," thank Larry Kenney as well. (Or curse him out; he is the voice of the Count.) You can even download the little "Sonny the Cocoa Puffs" bird and play along with him on your computer. Every time you win the game, he freaks out, practically having an epileptic seizure, screaming, "I'm coo-coo for Cocoa Puffs."

Where else have you heard Larry? Where haven't you heard him. His distinctive voice can be heard on promos on Comedy Central and on bumpers during USA Network movies. Kenney still auditions for many of his commercial roles, something Imus thinks is crazy given his stature in the world of voice-overs. Dick Cavett, who also does voice-overs, told Imus this is not unusual; advertisers want to see if you have the right tone for their product.

Kenney, like Bartlett, shows up late almost every day, according to Imus. When he is there, Kenney plays mostly dead guys on the program. Nixon, Elvis, Gen. George S. Patton Jr., and even Ross Perot are all attributed to Larry. (Actually, Ross Perot is alive; it's his political career that seems to be six feet under.) He also gets to impersonate other people still lurking about this mortal soil, including Sen. Edward M. Kennedy, David Brinkley, Walter Cronkite, and Paul Harvey. While on remotes, he usually likes to take on the persona of Reverend Jim, the drugged-out character from *Taxi* fame.

Kenney has also found some lucrative money in cartoons. While he is no Mel Blanc, the legendary voice of Bugs Bunny, he has played several notable animated characters. Larry provided two of the main voices for the cartoon series *Thundercats,* portraying "Lion-O" and "JackalMan" in 130 episodes that still air on the Cartoon Network. He also "starred" in *Silverhawks* as the character "Blue Grass" and portrayed "Leader of the Wind Demons" in the Christmas cartoon *The Life and Adventures of Santa Claus.*

For a while, Kenney called Westport, Connecticut, home, living in a "mansion" until his wife had kicked him out. That's the way he tells it, anyway.

He is now remarried; his MSNBC bio credits him with actually being the father of three kids and married to Carol Kenney, or "Mrs. Kenney Du Jour."

Kerri Kenney is Larry's oldest daughter, and she is what you might call a "gen-x celebrity." Kerri's credits start with MTV's *The State,* in which she was the lone woman, and include Comedy Central, where she stars in *Viva Variety.* On *Viva Variety* she plays "the Former Mrs. Laupin," sort of a European Cher takeoff. She is making the sweet money of commercials as well, having appeared as a tourist in a spot for Barq's Root Beer and as a cooking-school student for some dishwasher soap company. Kerri is a singer, too. She leads the chick band Cake Like.

# 19
## ROB BARTLETT
## IS A BIG FAT STAR

For our money, Rob Bartlett is the best part of the *Imus in the Morning* program. Back in the early 1980s, when listeners reached over and cranked the knob up on the radio to hear something better, it was Reverend Hargus or Crazy Bob. Now, more than likely, it's something with a Rob Bartlett touch to it that makes dials go higher.

His characters are widely varied. To one extreme is "Shecky Bhuta, the wacky Packey," a Pakistani stand-up comedian whose act is old jokes turned into Paki jokes. To the same extreme is "Buddy Miaggi," a Japanese stand-up comedian. His shtick is anti-American jokes, like "How many Americans does it take to change a lightbulb?"

"None, they are all too fat and lazy."

Those are a couple of his older characters, and they aren't all nationalistic stand-ups. To the other extreme are characters like singing "Bubba Clinton" and "Rush Limbaugh." "Bubba" hunkered down with "Hillary" to sing a duet, "I Got a Few Babes," to a Sonny and Cher tune, then belted one out with "Paula Jones" in a *Grease* takeoff, "Arkansas Nights." Rob's Bubba is strictly a solo on the fan favorite "Me and Paula Corbin Jones." He even gives regular peeks into Bubba's "diary," though usually with a jab at Imus tacked on for good measure. "Rush" gives commentary to Imus in Washington and sings as well. "The First Lady Is a Tramp" is a send-up of a Frank Sinatra tune.

In a bow to New Yorkers, always Imus's biggest audience, there is Sal Monella. Sal appears on the show from time to time, but you can count on a regular appearance at Christmastime. In an Imus fairy tale, Sal takes over for Santa. Mostly because Sal hit Santa over the head—*"badda-bing"*—with a pipe. It's the night before Christmas, Brooklyn style. Luckily, they manage to trot this bit out every holiday season.

Even if it's "Scottso Muni" or "Frank Bruno," while the real one is on the air being interviewed, the humor is all Bartlett. Now, Charles McCord writes many of the pieces you hear Larry Kenney do on the show or even some for Don in the past. Bartlett breaks the mold, though. He writes the majority of his own stuff. The song parodies are sung along with tracks from karaoke records.

While Bartlett provides great humor, it is not without controversy. In early 1994, Imus's popularity was growing by leaps and bounds. As Don's station list was growing, he would score big interviews with people like the president. The attention attracted articles, and the articles picked on some of Bartlett's work. Several times, Bartlett's parody "The First Lady Is a Tramp" was quoted, including one line that seemed to be a favorite: ". . . prefers to stand up when she urinates, that's why the first lady is a tramp."

It may have been strictly Bartlett's comedy, but it was attributed only to Imus's show. Of course, if Imus didn't endorse Bartlett's concept, it never would have made it on the show. Imus has not been shy about "blowing things up" or just not playing bits he doesn't like. It may seem in this case that Bartlett might have deserved to be singled out for his writing, but Don's name is at the top of the marquee. One thing you can say about Imus is that he is willing to take the heat for just about anything that airs on his program. Bear in mind, though, that Imus has reaped the rewards as well.

Not that Bartlett didn't hear about it at all. At one point he commented to the *New Haven Advocate* on the controversy. "That was meant as a satire," Bartlett recalls. "I was attempting to savage Rush as I had with 'I've Got Friends With White Faces.' It's like there are a lot of people who don't understand that [Imus pal Kinky Friedman's song] 'They Ain't Making Jews Like Jesus Anymore' is not an anti-Christian or anti-Semitic song. It's anything but; but it's very easy for people to assume that that's their anthem. But it's really a satire on the kind of people who would make that their anthem.

"I was really aghast at the things [Rush] was saying about the first lady on the air," he continues. Bartlett cites an episode of Rush's TV show in which he showed a picture of Socks, the White House cat, and Chelsea, "the White House dog," as a particularly "low blow."

Bartlett's bio goes back to the late seventies as a stand-up comedian. Actually, it goes back to his birth in Brooklyn and his being raised on Long Island. He would spend his time in high school listening to the I-Man on WNBC. On the stand-up stage, one of Bartlett's first comedy partners was none other than superstar Eddie Murphy. Along with another comedian, the trio formed a group called the Identical Triplets. It wasn't long before Eddie Murphy was off to work for NBC on *Saturday Night Live.*

Bartlett ended up in the same building, thanks to an old comedian friend named Mark Sheff, who was working as a producer for Imus. Bartlett started coming onto the show in 1986, with an imitation of New York–area ice-cream magnate Tom Carvel. In 1988, when the show went to WFAN, Bartlett was hired as a permanent contract player and has been a fixture for over ten years.

Before and during that time, he has continued to work on building his career in many different fields. He did a successful piece for Connecticut Public Television (CPTV) entitled *Rob Bartlett's Not for Profit TV.* It may not have made him a profit, but it did make him an award winner; he took home an Emmy.

The show itself was a send-up of public television. Bartlett set his sights on public TV standards like sponsorships by big companies trying to get a little PR; cooking shows, goofy painters, Ken Burns's documentaries, and even pledge breaks. The amazing part is that CPTV actually ran a real pledge drive around the show.

Much like Larry Kenney and Charles McCord, Bartlett has found some voice work on the side. Rob has done spots for NYNEX and Dunkin' Donuts. He has appeared in several Wendy's commercials opposite Dave Thomas, including one where he teaches Dave how to "speak" hockey.

What you won't find in any of his published biographies

was that Bartlett spent time working as a commentator on wrestling broadcasts back in 1993. He even finished ninth in that year's fan voting as Worst Color Commentator. The Macho Man Randy Savage took the top nod, according to a wrestling Web site. Bartlett may have gotten the gig from his charity work. He was teamed up with World Wrestling Federation (WWF) top man Vince McMahon to call the play-by-play for a charity softball event in 1991. It was the start of a beautiful friendship.

His stand-up act has taken him to college-campus auditoriums and to television. He has hit cities like Providence, Rhode Island, and Washington, D.C., with his "laugh tsunami." He even did the Las Vegas lounge circuit. A Boston show was an Imus fan's delight. He appeared on the same bill with Delbert McClinton. Delbert is a fabulous singer and one of the Imus show's most popular guests. Rob has appeared on *Late Night With Conan O'Brian* and *Late Night With David Letterman,* plus VH-1, MTV, and several comedy specials. He has also made a few bucks selling a CD of some of his bits at his stand-up shows. Entitled *All You Need Is Rob,* the CD is a classic. The original Sal Monella's "Night Before Christmas" and my favorite Bartlett song, "Big Butted Woman," is on it—if you can find it.

Rob accepted a challenge and took on his biggest project ever in the spring of 1998 when he created his show, *Rob Bartlett in Have a Nice Life, a Big Fat Comedy.* The all-new stage show played for three weeks off-Broadway in Stamford, Connecticut's Rich Forum. The plot: an overweight stand-up comedian turns forty and juggles his family life. Quite a stretch. While, as a result, Rob made few appearances on the program and missed a road trip, his show was a success. It played so well in the "sticks," to use a show-business term, that it premiered on Thursday, October 15, 1998, on Broadway. Unfortunately, its run was all too brief. It closed the weekend it opened.

Even though *Have a Nice Life* is loosely based on his own experiences, you won't find him talking a lot about them. Most celebrities shield their home lives, and Bartlett is no exception. What I can tell you is that he is married to what must be a wonderful, caring, understanding woman named Sharon. Rob still lives on Long Island and is a father of at least one boy, who shares Dad's sense of humor whether he knows it or not. A few peeks into his home life will tell you that Bartlett is a cigar aficionado. In fact, he gave them out on the birth of his son. His leisure activities include surfing with a Power Mac, watching laser disks with a lean toward James Bond, and playing a little Nintendo.

The addition of Imus on MSNBC has continued to make Rob Bartlett a multimedia star once again. Now you get to see bits like "Arkansas Nights" on the stage at the TCF radiothon, though that's not always a benefit. If you watch the "Bartlette" assigned the duties of playing Paula Jones to his Bubba, she takes constant peeks at a crib sheet in her hand, just to make sure she remembers the words.

The wonderful people who put the television side together have worked with Bartlett to produce some great moments. Several times we were allowed to go behind the scenes with Rob at his stage shows, such as *Rob Bartlett Is a Big Fat Idiot*. It's great fun to watch Bartlett speak of himself as a team player and call his group a family. Moments later, watch him berate someone over the most minor of details or lisping around singing show tunes.

The best of the MSNBC content, though, has been the story of Mark from Milwaukee. If you don't know the character, Mark is the most obsessed Imus fan alive. The video is the creation of Jeremy Newberger, with Bartlett in the role of Mark, who has our deranged (or perhaps misunderstood) fan misconstruing a conversation with Imus and believing he has been invited to see the I-Man. He loads up for his trip carefully: cowboy hat, bandanna tied around his neck, a black Tornado jacket, and carrying a copy of *Two Guys, Four Corners*.

He is not greeted with the greatest of respect during his journey, however. The parking-lot attendant comes after him with a bat, he is ushered out of the Kaufman Astoria studios, and even the corner store can't give him a refill of Southwest Salsa after he drinks his on a stoop. His support never wavers for Imus, though. It's a well-edited piece, a must-see. Check it out during the "Best of Imus" or at MSNBC's Web site.

Of all the Imus crew, Bartlett is probably the most accessible to the fans. His travels with his stand-up act have taken him all along the eastern seaboard, greeting the fans that tune in every week. He also has his own Web site, www.robshow.com, which he uses to communicate with his fans, not only about the Imus show but about all his entertainment work. Rob keeps fans informed of tour dates, checks out listener letters, and brings us the Road Warrior Diaries.

The Road Warrior Diaries may be the most "inside the Imus show" thing you will ever read. As the cast and crew take trips around the country for various remote broadcasts, Rob gets his number 2 pencil out and jots down a few interesting things about the trip, sometimes even accompanied by pictures. The missives from the front give us keen insights, like the first impressions of Don's new Executive Jet, called *I-Force One* by those in the know. For some odd reason, comments keep coming up about the impending death of Imus, or wishes thereof.

Bartlett routinely trades barbs with fans in the Internet news group alt.fan.don-imus. Thanks to longtime Imus fan Jack Schnapper, Bartlett actually has his own news group, alt.fan.rob-bartlett, the only other Imus-related news group. Rob "brings something to the table" in his visits. In one of his longest posts he defended the Imus Ranch, but his tone usually isn't so serious. Instead, he'll talk about his commercial career with Wendy's or a close encounter with Stephen King during the trip to Bangor, Maine.

Now, we could write his E-mail address right here and let him be deluged with letters (if three can be considered a deluge), but we won't. While Rob has not hidden from people, there is not only an etiquette issue involved; there is the fun of the chase. Now that you know where to look for him, go post in the news group and see what happens. You have the clues.

# 20
## ROUND UP THE POSSE

**I**t's not just the contributions of Imus, McCord, Kenney, and Bartlett that make *Imus in the Morning* great; it is a fantastic cast of talented people who work alongside these radio gods. Here is the 411 on the rest of the Imus posse:

### AL ROSENBERG

Al Rosenberg may have been covered fairly well in the chapter "Imus Versus Stern," the NBC Years. Even with all the talk, then, there are a few more things you might want to know about the third voice guy in Imus's stable.

After working with Stern for a few years, Rosenberg left the show to go out on his own. He even ended up competing with his two friends with a radio show. Something unique, though, was Rosenberg's venture into television. He was a puppet named Bob on the short-lived *Fox After Breakfast* program that was done live in New York.

Now, with his puppet days behind him, he is back on the Imus program. Probably a good thing, too. He helps fill some of the void that occurs with Rob working on his Broadway show. "Earl C. Watkins" isn't back, but "C. Vernon Mason" seems to be Al's favorite voice, as he calls in to the I-Man to talk about issues of the day or just trash Rob.

### MIKE BREEN

Far more than just the primary sportscaster of the *Imus in the Morning*, Mike Breen is a talented and busy sports anchor and play-by-play man. Breen divides his non-Imus time between NBC Sports and the Madison Square Garden network (MSG). At NBC, you may have seen Breen doing play-by-play for the 1996 Summer Olympics, the WNBA, and the NFL or hosting *SportsDesk.* Over at MSG, Mike Breen is the television voice of one of the premier franchises in the NBA, the New York Knicks.

Much to Imus's benefit, Breen inherited the Knicks television job from Marv Albert, who resigned his post after a court case with a former lover that made a little news. Breen moved up from the radio play-by-play job, where he was heralded by critics for his solid work with Walt Frasier. Imus still gives Breen a hard time for being a "homer" and rooting for the Knicks and probably always will.

His current term as Imus sportscaster began in 1991, but it's not the only one. Breen did sports during the Imus show when it was still broadcast at WNBC. Notably, in the interim, 1988–91, Imus sports was hosted by Don Criqui, longtime NBC sportscaster who switched to CBS Sports in 1998.

Breen has an alter ego, and his name is "Bill from White Plains," who will occasionally call in, strangely only when Breen is on the road. "Bill" will talk sports with the I-Man and usually has less than flattering comments about Warner Wolf.

Some of Breen's trademarks on the Imus program include trying to slip fake sound bites past the I-Man. He will drag out five- or six-year-old clips of various ballplayers and try to slip them in as today's comments. Imus can usually stop Breen, but like Wayne Gretsky, he will eventually slip a few past Imus the goalkeeper, which makes it all the more funny.

Breen can get his share of digs in on Imus as well. One of the funniest occurred when Breen was reporting on how Deirdre and her friends had recently sung "The Star-Spangled Banner" at Shea Stadium before a Mets game. The accompanying sound bite featured several off-key kindergartners belting out "and the home of the braaaaaave." This is from the same man who also said that the proposal of marriage between Imus and Coleman actually came from Deirdre and played the sound bite from a commercial saying, "Grandpa, can I marry you?"

## WARNER WOLF

Wolf became a New York icon for saying, "Let's go to the video-tape." He might owe his latest New York incarnation to John Donald Imus. After leaving WCBS in New York for the friendly confines of Washington, D.C., for a few years, Wolf came back to New York as the fill-in sports host of the *Imus in the Morning* program. He had the free time because he had lost his job in D.C. after some on-air controversy.

Imus welcomed Wolf back and had him fill in for Mike Breen at every opportunity when Breen was on the road with football or the Knicks. When WCBS was looking to form a new news team after a mass firing à la WNBC Radio in 1977, there was Warner Wolf, scoring big on the *Imus in the Morning* program and tailor-made to take over the new job. In fact, Wolf credits Imus with his return to New York television, telling the *New York Daily News,* "I think if I hadn't got the shot with Imus, I never would've gotten that call from Channel 2."

In the harassment category, Wolf usually gets it from Imus for his extremely lame, made-up sports "actualities," sound bites of the players and coaches. He also caught some grief from the I-Man for his trip to Wimbledon. Now, we all know Imus travels better than first-class all the way: private jets, the best hotel rooms, and limo service. Wolf took the package tour bus trips and buffet meals, not to the satisfaction of the I-Man, who felt one of New York's premier sportscasters should travel in style.

## BERNARD McGUIRK

Anyone who has called 1-800-370-IMUS to try to speak with Imus knows this man at the other end of the phone. Bernard McGuirk is the one you have to try to get by to talk to Imus on the air. Bernie is much more than a call screener, though. As the executive producer of the *Imus in the Morning* program, he is responsible for keeping the show rolling. He makes sure the guests are on the phone or in the studio at the proper time. He keeps track of the interns, who keep track of the boss's coffee, among other things.

McGuirk is also an integral character on the show in his own right. If Charles McCord is the good angel sitting on Imus's shoulder, trying to keep Don from crossing the line, Bernard is the devil, trying to bring out the worst in the I-Man. He is the most cynical of the gang, which is saying a lot for this group. On his best days he will throw in comments that prompt Imus to scold him verbally while waving his hand looking for more from behind the glass.

From his perch on the stool next to Lou, he deals out his barbs, either as himself or as his alter egos, "Cardinal O'Connor" and "Maya Angelou." The cardinal, over from the archdiocese of New York, is in theory there to read the New York State Lottery numbers. However, what he usually does is launch into attacks on Imus, "Ya wrinkled-up old fool, ya," or McCord, "Ya jackbooted Nazi." Almost always, you can count on the cardinal to wrap up with a "which doesn't belong and why." The game features three contestants; the I-Man has to pick which of the three doesn't fit.

Maya Angelou is the famous African-American poet who, in character form, is brought to life by Bernie. Bernie reads poems, making each one a "hate whitey" story. Of course, if you listen to frequent Imus guests Stephan Dweck and Monteria Ivey, authors of *Baby, All Those Curves and Me With No Brakes: 500 New No-Fail Pick-Up Lines for Men and Women,* every African-American character McGuirk does sounds like Buckwheat or Kingfish.

McGuirk has made a name for himself with his on-the-scene reports. Investigative Bernie has visited the scene of Judge Harold Rothwax's troubles with New York City, pointing out the chalk outline supposedly of the judge and suggesting the judge just came from the liquor store. He also spent time in the Bronx, interviewing locals. (He called them "natives.") This feature had McGuirk asking the locals around Yankee Stadium if it should be moved out of the Bronx, to New Jersey or Manhattan. Of course, in true McGuirk style, he did it in fatigues and gave out forty-ounce beers in paper bags.

Bernard McGuirk wasn't always Imus's producer, though. Actually, he started off working at 30 Rock as an intern at 66 WNBC-AM and on the *NBC Nightly News* program before he became producer of the Imus program in 1983. He has had a few outside activities. Bernie has done stand-up in the New York and Boston areas a few times. He was also chosen, along with Laura Ingraham and George Carlin, by Tony Hendra to conduct a test of micro-brew beers for *New York* magazine.

### LOU RUFFINO

Lou Ruffino is another of the men behind the glass. He's the man who makes the switches work and part of the small audience (usually just he and McGuirk) that Imus plays to. Ruffino is responsible for all the sound on the show, which means Imus is the first person to jump on Lou when a wrong tape plays or something doesn't run right when he cues it. Ruffino is ready to defend himself, though. After all, equipment isn't perfect, and he is not about to take any crap from the I-Man.

Ruffino actually came to the Imus show as a holdover from 1050 WFAN. That doesn't mean he was instantly accepted. In fact, after having put the "duck" on hiatus, Imus brought it back so Ruffino would pay attention. According to his MSNBC bio, Lou has switched places with Imus twice, in what must have been an "I can do this better than you can" fight.

Lou is the Imus program's resident expert on music, too. He can probably quote any lyrics, from the songs sung by Tony Bennett to those of the Foo Fighters. When Imus has a question about a Stones tour, for example, you can bet he'll turn to Ruffino.

### MARK CHERNOFF

In a strange twist of fate, Mark Chernoff has had the opportunity to be program director at the station carrying Howard Stern, then at the station carrying Don Imus. Talk about a job that would give you a few Maalox moments! Of course, he has taken his share of abuse from both of them. In exchange, he has gotten his share of acclaim in the broadcasting industry. Chernoff is featured on an educational tape touting secrets of program directors.

He also seems to be head of the Imus radio network, dealing with calls from stations around the country, requests for custom recordings by Imus, or even complaints about topics of the week. He also takes care of the technical end on the road—microphones, phone lines, and all the little things that need doing.

You can occasionally see Mark filling in behind the glass when Bernie is off or on the road, taking phone calls from listeners and abuse from Imus. Imus will tell you, though, that Chernoff is the best program director he has ever worked for, with Bob Pittman ranking second.

## JANE METZLER — NEWS EDITOR

Jane spends her mornings behind a typewriter, producing the news for the *Imus in the Morning* program. The blond-haired Metzler compiles the New York news and national news for Charles McCord while he sits at the right hand of the I-Man every morning.

Metzler, from New Mexico, took over several years ago and continues to fill in for Charles whenever he is out or on "Best of Imus" days.

## DAYNA CAVANAUGH — ASSOCIATE PRODUCER, *IMUS IN THE MORNING*

After going through a batch of secretaries that, according to rumors, would make the Mormon Tabernacle Choir look small, Imus has found Dayna Cavanaugh. Cavanaugh handles phone calls, ranch stuff, and all the administrative material for Imus, even carrying the title of producer of the show.

According to Imus, the secretary problem seemed to stem from letting Bernie and Lou do the hiring. At least one former secretary would dispute that, though. Angela Maron, who had held down the desk at one time, appeared on the talent show Imus held and made him out to be the king of all evil.

## TERRY IRVING — EXECUTIVE PRODUCER, *IMUS ON MSNBC*

The only man who can say he spent regular time working with Ted Koppel and Don Imus is Terry Irving, executive producer of *Imus on MSNBC*. Irving is a former acclaimed *Nightline* producer who left the television business to try his hand in new media. He was lured back into television and, with the siren song of MSNBC, now gets to combine his interest in the Internet and his television-producing skills into one job.

Irving's primary job is taking the brunt of Imus's abuse on the television side. Imus is always ready to lash out at him for something, mostly for eating doughnuts. Irving does come through, though, helping to bring the stable of NBC correspondents to the show. Irving also "gets the tape" better than a magician pulling scarves. It seems that every time Imus utters the words "Ask Terry to get a tape of . . .", he has it ready to roll.

Irving is also the boss of the rest of the MSNBC gang, including producers Jeff Green, who is in charge of many "Best of Imus" programs, and Jeremy Newberger, the Internet guy; plus director Curtis Tate.

## Jeremy Newberger — Associate Producer, *Imus on MSNBC*

Newberger is the guru of *Imus on MSNBC* on the Internet. After working as a page and conducting tours at 30 Rock in New York, he latched on as a production assistant on the brand-new cable venture. Newberger began distinguishing himself with his editing skills. The talented producer has put together many memorable video segments; at the start they were "Best of Imus" clips from the program. He went on to comedic short segments, such as "Imus's Dance Party," when Butterbean's head is the bouncing ball following the words YMCA and A-B-C while out-of context clips show the gang dancing along to the music.

He has made the transition to producer of scripted segments usually starring Rob Bartlett. After several trips behind the scenes at Rob's various shows, he produced the story of "Mark From Milwaukee."

Newberger also rules the imus.msnbc.com Web site. In addition to having video clips on demand, like the "Mark From Milwaukee" segment, the site features original content about the program, such as links to guests' sites and bios of the cast and crew. Newberger is rarely absent from the Internet chat; most mornings find him on as Jeremy MSNBC.

As talented as Newberger is, that doesn't keep Imus from lashing out at him. One morning he came under attack as a loser, who only needed a "Yamaha" and a raincoat to look like a Hassidic Jew. Most of the time, however, he gets credit from Don for his taped pieces, and Imus has even called Newberger's "Best of Imus" sometimes better than the real show.

# PART IV

# THE LISTS

# 21
# THE GUEST LIST

Imagine, if you will, a roast of Imus. An imaginary dinner with a group of Imus's closest friends and associates who know the most interesting things in his life. If you like, you can imagine a wake following the demise of our I-Man, if that's your preference.

The room is filled with well-wishers, but who would you put at the top of the list? Who would tell the best stories? Here are my picks for some of Don's most intriguing guests, friends, and associates.

## TIM RUSSERT

**Day job:** executive vice president and Washington bureau chief, NBC News; host of *Meet the Press.*

**Imus relationship:** Mr. Russert is one of the closest Imus advisers on the political scene as well as one of the most popular guests on the show. Tim may appear as often as needed when Washington is topping the national news.

**Why he's on the list:** Mr. Russert is one of the Imus's most entertaining guests. His appearances are always in the Imus style, entertaining but informative. He probably tops the list because he can tear Imus up with the best of them, leaving him in the dust.

**Most memorable appearances:** Two great guest appearances by Russert stand out. The first was right after Green Bay won the Super Bowl, much to the disappointment of Imus, who was rooting for Bill Parcells and his New England Patriots. Sitting right across from the I-Man, Russert shamed Imus into wearing a Wisconsin cheesehead and made him repeat, "Congratulations to the Green Bay Packers and the cheeseheads. And when you're my age, you like cheese. It's easy to chew."

Russert was back in the middle of the Clinton-Lewinsky scandal during Imus's visit to Washington, D.C. The jovial newsman arrived at the remote with two lifesized cutouts: one of Don peeking out from behind President Clinton's coattails and the other featuring former White House intern Monica Lewinsky in an Auto Body Express denim work shirt.

Tim Russert even brought Imus to his own turf and got the best of Don. Not long after Don admitted to a lapse in his vegetarianism while on jury duty, he appeared on Tim Russert's CNBC show. Russert presented him with two giant-sized hot dogs and challenged him to eat them. Don chowed them down as the show was wrapping up. Which proves that Russert falls into that select class of Imus guests who gets to see the true Imus and harass him endlessly.

## BERNADETTE CASTRO

**Day job:** New York State parks commissioner

**Imus relationship:** longtime advertiser and friend

**Why she's on the list:** She knows the show's history, and she's still involved in it.

**Most memorable appearances:** If you didn't live in the New York area during the 1960s, 1970s or 1980s, you might say, "Who is this?" Ms. Castro is heir to the Castro Convertible couch-that-pulls-out-into-a-bed fortune. Bernadette used to be their spokeswoman, both as a child, showing how easy it was, and later as the big boss. Now, being connected with politics as New York State parks commissioner, she brings to the table a couple of important things.

First would be the history of Don from the early New York years. She has been an occasional regular on the show for years—always welcome but never a pest. Bernadette has the

## Top Ten Most Entertaining Guests
### (as chosen by the author)

1. Tim Russert
2. Jeff Greenfield
3. Butterbean (boxer Eric Esh)
4. Robert W. Morgan
5. Willie Nelson
6. George Carlin
7. Laura Ingraham
8. The God Squad (Rabbi Gelman and Monsignor Hartman)
9. Al Roker
10. Bill Parcells

knowledge that comes from having been a primary target of the occasional Imus attack.

Second, she has helped Imus with his late-found legitimacy as a photographer. After *Two Guys, Four Corners,* she was responsible for seeking out Imus to photograph Niagara Falls. The photograph would go on to grace the cover of the New York State parks guide. Of course, if she should decide to run for higher political office than the appointed position she holds, Imus's involvement wouldn't hurt. I expect that Ms. Castro would receive the full endorsement of the *Imus in the Morning* program no matter what she ran for.

Let's hope Ms. Castro brings her spouse as well. Dr. Peter Guida is a renowned New York surgeon and the man Don credits for bringing him safely through his lung surgery.

## KINKY FRIEDMAN

**Day job:** Singer, songwriter, and author

**Imus relationship:** friend

**Why he's on the list:** Kinky is another throwback to the early years, often having drinks with Don at the Lone Star Café in New York.

**Most memorable appearances:** The Kinkster, as he is known, plays to a totally different facet of Imus's mind. As documented throughout this book, Don's interests from his late teens included making music. Kinky's music is probably the kind he would be making today. Kinky has made some strange country tunes his own, from *"They Ain't Makin' Jews Like Jesus Anymore"* to *"Waitress, Dear Waitress (come sit on my face . . .)."* Like Imus, Kinky is an author as well. He published *Roadkill* in 1997, a murder mystery involving legendary country singer Willie Nelson.

Kinky brought Nelson onto the show once, and it was a fantastic appearance. Willie completely opened up and got the crew to sing along, becoming the chorus in a rendition of "Hello, Wall." The legendary singer even traded jokes with the I-Man. Nelson, after reminding Imus how Elvis died in the toilet, asked Don if he knew what Elvis's last words were. With a shake of the head, Willie dryly uttered the answer: "Corn?"

Don't be surprised to find Kinky on a loser guest day, though. Sometimes Kinky just doesn't get it done on the comedy side, though you can always count on him to be outrageous. For example, he told MSNBC his goal was to burn down Cuba, one cigar at a time.


## GERALDO RIVERA

**Day job:** host of CNBC's *Rivera Live*

**Imus relationship:** friend since the early seventies

**Why he's on the list:** He once walked out of his job at WABC in New York over a story about Imus.

**Most memorable appearances:** Aside from the big blowout with his bosses at WABC (check out the chapter "Welcome to 30 Rock" for the whole story), Imus and Geraldo have long been New York icons. Not one specific appearance comes to mind for Rivera, but they share a lot of common ground.

Remember the *Imus Plus* television show? Well, Geraldo should. Legend has it that he was the announcer for the show back in the seventies. Most people know Rivera from his national talk show, his CNBC program, or even from the Al Capone vault fiasco. Rivera really got his start in New York not long after Imus. In the early 1970s, Rivera was a reporter for WABC in New York and broke a famous scandal over the Willowbrook School for the mentally retarded. He was also a staffer on *20/20,* and *Good Morning America.*

Rivera could likely dish some great dirt on Imus, especially the early years. It would be interesting to plot the rise and fall of Geraldo Rivera along with that of Imus. Not that the two had any direct effect on each other, but they have both had several similar peaks and valleys in their lives. Both were recognized at one time in the early 1970s as top dogs in their respective fields in New York. Both Rivera and Imus have been divorced, been faced with the loss of their jobs, and had to backtrack to get ahead (Imus to Cleveland, Geraldo to the

Capone vault). Now they both seem to be enjoying enormous success, with Geraldo having signed a long-term deal with NBC News.

## Mike Lupica

**Day job:** sports columnist

**Imus relationship:** close friend

**Why he's on the list:** At one time, Mike Lupica was the I-Man's best friend (next to McCord, of course).

**Most memorable appearances:** Lupica is another person who has enjoyed the media spotlight. He makes frequent television appearances on ESPN's *Sports Reporters* and hosts the *Mike Lupica Show* on ESPN2. As a sportswriter for the *New York Daily News* and the *National,* among other papers, Lupica is good for an occasional quotation from the I-Man in his columns.

Of course, he is good for a lot more than that. He knows the Imus family intimately. He is the coauthor of *The Fred Book* along with Fred Imus. His most memorable contribution to the show occurred when Don's lung collapsed. Lupica helped anchor in the studio while Imus phoned in from his bedside. He still calls occasionally, but unfortunately not nearly as frequently as he used to. He is another one of those guests who "gets it done."

There was a time when Lupica was actually a WFAN employee. The powers that be had brought "the Lip" in to cohost a midday sports show. Since its inception, WFAN's midday programming has probably been its most inconsistent, with former New York sportscaster Bill Mazer hosting lunch at Mickey Mantle's restaurant at one time. So the Lip was teamed up with Len Berman, WNBC-TV sportscaster and sometime contributor to the *Today* show. Of course, Imus set about to cause controversy, and, unlike with *Mike and the Mad Dog,* he may have succeeded, because it wasn't long before the team was broken up. (See the chapter "Sports Radio" for more on this event.)

## Jeff Greenfield

**Day job:** political analyst, CNN

**Imus relationship:** admired commentator and frequent contributor

**Why he's on the list:** a payback for a dinner gone bad

**Most memorable appearances:** It would be fun to invite Jeff Greenfield to the party just to see what would happen to the invitation. Greenfield once took a chance and did the unthinkable: He invited Don to a dinner party at his home. What did Imus do? Gave it away on the air to a listener. Unfortunately for the listener, Greenfield had to withdraw his invitation.

Jeff Greenfield is, probably more than Tim Russert or the *Boston Globe*'s Mike Barnicle, Imus's most trusted news adviser. Back when the Marv Albert sex case was ongoing, it was Greenfield whom Imus turned to when faced with a dilemma. *New York Daily News* columnist Sidney Zion had given our favorite shock jock the name of Marv's accuser in exchange for Imus's agreeing to announce it on the air. Greenfield became the "professor" in helping Imus decide if he should "name names." The final verdict: The name was not given on the Imus show; it was only to be leaked to someone later that same day.

I wouldn't say Greenfield consulted Imus when weighing a move from ABC News to CNN in 1997, but Imus gave his opinion, anyway. The decision was ultimately Greenfield's, though. He is now chief political analyst for the Cable News Network.

## Martha Stewart

**Day job:** queen of home crafting and cooking

**Imus relationship:** occasional guest

**Why she's on the list:** Imus's Connecticut neighbor

**Most memorable appearances:** Martha lives near the I-Man in Connecticut and has offered to have the Imuses over for dinner. Don, having no life except for following Deirdre around and watching television, declined.

## Delbert McClinton

**Day job:** singer

**Imus relationship:** friend

**Why he's on the list:** provided the "Hate Radio Rodeo" house band.

**Most memorable appearances:** Delbert has long been admired by Imus for some great songs, for example: *"I'm With You," "Lie No Better,"* and *"Better Off With the Blues."* He got a chance to sing those songs on the program, too. When Don and Fred put on the first "Hate Radio Rodeo" in 1996, they asked Delbert and his band to provide the music that rocked the joint. Delbert has also appeared on such programs as *Austin City Limits* and worked with the Beatles, teaching Paul McCartney to play harmonica. (Wouldn't it be nice just to talk to him about that?)

There has been what can best be described as a suspicion among some Imus fans that Imus appeared in a Delbert McClinton music video. The song, the Beatles hit "Come Together," is set in a darkened nightclub, with patrons along the walls and seated at tables. At one table near the front is a man in a turban, and just behind him, is it Don Imus? Well, the shot takes less than a second, and the man looks like Imus.

My opinion, though, is that it *is* him, and either Don did it as a favor to Delbert, or Delbert did it as a payback to Don for helping plug his records all the time. Wanting the official word, though, I asked the Delbert Fan Club. They sent me on to another person, who sent me the E-mail message "I asked Delbert and Wendy, and they tell me that Don Imus is not in the video."

## Joseph Abboud

**Day job:** designer

**Imus relationship:** supplier of custom-designed clothes to the Auto Body Express

**Why he's on the list:** the clothes

**Most memorable appearances:** The designer to the stars has appeared a couple of times to be grilled about the western clothes he designed for the Auto Body Express. The appearance that stands out, however, is the time, just before the birth of Wyatt, that Mr. Abboud dropped by to give Imus a present. Now, again and again, Imus said on the air that he did not want presents for little Wyatt. That did not impede Mr. Abboud. He presented Imus with some artwork.

The picture was a poster-size charcoal drawing of Imus looking over his shoulder, wearing a four-corners jacket and a set of wings. You would think Imus would have been a little appreciative, especially from a friend. But then, that wouldn't be Don. He lashed out at Abboud for the hideous picture, and you can bet it will never get near Wyatt, much less over his bed, as the designer suggested.


## LAURA INGRAHAM

**Day job:** right-wing political pundit

**Imus relationship:** frequent guest and sparring partner

**Why she's on the list:** the cow

**Most memorable appearances:** Laura Ingraham can pop up in a discussion almost anywhere. The blond bombshell of the right wing is a fan of the show in a big way. She has appeared in the MSNBC chat to just hack around with the gang. When Bernard McGuirk was seen live in front of the White House, she had no problem driving by in her little green truck. This is the kind of guest Laura Ingraham is.

Her biggest claim to fame now is having Fred name a cow after her. Laura and Fred have a love-hate relationship. One morning, after Imus finished talking with Laura, Fred phoned with a question. Laura the cow could stick her tongue in her nose, and he wanted to know if Laura the person could do the same. She was back on the phone in a flash, and the test was made. Sorry to say, her tongue didn't make it. At least she said she couldn't get "her own" tongue in her nose.

## DAN RATHER

**Day job:** managing editor and anchor, *CBS Evening News.*

**Imus relationship:** media-elite guest. Both work for CBS.

**Why he's on the list:** He could go off at any moment.

**Most memorable appearances:** Dan Rather has gone where no man has before. Not with the Starship Enterprise but with the Imus brothers on a photo shoot. The memorable appearance would actually end up on CBS's *48 Hours.*

Following the release of *Two Guys, Four Corners,* the veteran journalist took a trip with the Brothers Imus back to Monument Valley for a photo exposition. The gear was loaded on the *I-Jet,* and off they flew for the weekend. Rather, always the professional journalist, actually paid the equivalent airfare for him and the crew.

The boys strolled through the desert, but the adventure occurred at the end of the trip. The fabulous *I-Jet* landed on a little-used air-strip in northern New Mexico and taxied off the concrete runway to the tarmac taxiway, where it got embedded in the tar, which had melted in the New Mexico sun. Luckily, Fred had remained to watch the takeoff and helped them break into the rental Jeeps they had left. The gang drove a hundred miles and flew back in time for another plane to whisk them back to New York.

In less than twenty-four hours the MSNBC gang brought the world the tape of the stuck plane. The calls started coming in right away as well. New Mexico senator John McCain was one of the first to call Imus, thanking him for falling for the old "plane stuck in the tar" trick and contributing to the New Mexico economy with the crews they had to hire to remove the jet.

## MICHAEL LYNNE

**Day job:** president and chief executive officer, New Line Cinema

**Imus relationship:** longtime Imus attorney

**Why he's on the list:** He knows where the bodies are buried.

**Most memorable appearances:** I don't recall ever hearing Mike Lynne call in to the program, but he has been spoken of. Imus will mention him in many contexts: Mike the friend, Mike the lawyer, or Mike the studio head.

Imus's novel *God's Other Son* was dedicated to one person—not to his brother, wives, or daughters but to Michael Lynne, both the 1981 version and the reissue in 1992. While Lynne rated a mention in the opening comments of the 1981 publication as well, the 1992 edition tells how Lynne helped Imus through the tough times of his drug and alcohol abuse. Imus praised Lynne for his honesty in telling Imus he had a problem and his support in overcoming it.

Lynne has been through it all as Imus's attorney. It's hard to say how much legal work Lynne actually does for Imus now, with his job running New Line Cinema, but it wasn't always the case. Even in his days in Cleveland, when he would threaten people, he would refer to Lynne. If Kenneth Starr ever needed the dirt on Imus, this is an attorney-client privilege he would love to crack.

## ESTHER "LOBSTER" NEWBERG

**Day Job:** agent, International Creative Management

**Imus relationship:** Imus's literary agent

**Why she's on the list:** deserves a free meal for the hell she's been through.

**Most memorable appearances:** Usually it's memorable talk about Newberg that comes to mind. She might not appear on the show often—if she does, it's on the phone—but her name is taken in vain all the time. Of course, she's referred to by another fish term aside from Lobster, and that would be Little Shrimp. Pretty bad treatment for someone who worked for Robert Kennedy.

She is one of the most powerful agents in the business, though. Aside from the Imus brothers, she represents Kinky Friedman, Sarah the duchess of York, Patricia Cornwell, and Caroline Kennedy Schlossberg, just to name a few. When there is a publishing story in the news, many reporters cite Newberg as a source. Most likely because if she doesn't represent them directly, she represents someone they know.

Of course, this list may never be complete. It would be fun to invite President Clinton to see how he took the speech from hell a few years later. Perhaps maybe George Carlin for laughs. Maybe even Howard Stern to see if he could actually give Imus a little credit. How about Harriet Imus, or one of his daughters, to find out about Imus's home life?

Then, even if I did invite them, what's the chance they would all fit around my kitchen table?

# 22

# THE RADIO CHARACTERS

This is probably the most complete list you will come across of the many characters who have appeared on *Imus in the Morning*. Some are current, some are just for occasional use, and some are just for special occasions. Since a detailed list of every single character who ever appeared even once on the show would be tedious as well as overly long, here's a look at the majors. The performer who voices the character is given in parenthesis following the character's name.

## CURRENT CHARACTERS

### Richard Nixon (Larry Kenney)
The former president of the United States is "Imus in Washington Senior Political Analyst"; his essays generally emanate from the Dick Scope. Nixon has been a staple of the show for years, usually attacking the current administration. He went on hiatus for a short while after the real Nixon's death, but what's wrong with a Dead Dick?
*Famous line:* sings the *Imus in the Morning* jingle.
*In real life:* deceased former president

### Gen. George S. Patton (Larry Kenney)
The general is the head military strategist of the show. He will divulge plans to take out whoever is currently on the Imus hot seat.
*Famous line:* "Give me a full military strike on those lights, Private."
*In real life:* deceased former general

### Rush Limbaugh (Rob Bartlett)

Rush talks and sings about politics. Think of the real Rush taken to the next degree. At one time, he was discontinued by the Imus show, but he made a comeback once the Clinton-intern scandal broke. He was the character who caused much of the controversy by singing "The First Lady Is a Tramp."

*Famous line:* sings "I've Got Friends With White Faces."

*In real life:* syndicated talk-radio host appearing on hundreds of stations nationwide

### Walter Cronkite (Larry Kenney)

The veteran journalist Cronkite delivers fake news from the *Imus in Washington* network newsroom.

*Famous line:* "Jesus, what a f\*\*\*ing mess!"

*In real life:* former anchor of *CBS Evening News*

### Wilfred Brimley (Larry Kenney)

The old-timer with an odd urge. On behalf of the Quaker Oats people, Mr. Brimley offers tips on preparing your oatmeal, usually along with basting a turkey. Unfortunately, he usually recommends warming it from the inside, in an intimate, if not totally perverted, manner. Okay, he advocates having sex with the turkey. All right?

*Famous line:* "It's the right thing to do."

*In real life:* actor and spokesman

### Scott Muni (Rob Bartlett)

The famous New York deejay reports on entertainment, like the current Rolling Stones tour or the Grammy Awards. In a "pseudoremote" he once reported, "The tractor-trailer trucks containing Garth Brooks's ego have arrived."

*Famous line:* "So me, Grace Slick, and Tommy Tune were . . ."

*In real life:* former host on WNEW-FM in New York, "where rock lives"

### Paul Harvey (Larry Kenney)

Another *Imus in Washington* correspondent, the pseudo-Harvey delivers his take on the days events.

*Famous line:* "And now, the rest of the story."

*In real life:* still doing his reports on the ABC Radio Network.

## Ten Most Popular Characters
### (as chosen by the author)

1. The Right Reverend Dr. Billy Sol Hargus

2. Blind Mississippi White Boy Pig-Feets Dupree

3. Crazy Bob

4. Geraldo Santana Banana

5. Gen. George S. Patton

6. Cardinal O'Connor

7. Bubba Clinton

8. Walter Cronkite

9. Earl C. Watkins and Mark from Milwaukee (tie)

### John Cardinal O'Connor (Bernard McGuirk)

If they are not Irish and Catholic, they are badmouthed by the cardinal, whose official job on the *Imus in the Morning* program is to read the New York State Lotto numbers. Often refers to Imus as "You schmuck ya . . ." and McCord as a "Nazi."

*Famous line:* "Which doesn't belong and why?"

*In real life:* Catholic cardinal who runs the archdiocese of New York

### The Right Reverend Dr. Billy Sol Hargus (Don Imus)

One of Don's first characters, if not the first. The reverend runs the First Church of the Gooey Death and Discount House of Worship, which sells such items as flights on Hebrew Airlines and the wings of "Him." Hargus (also spelled Hargis in the early years) was the first character heard on WNBC when Imus returned from Cleveland in 1979 as "God's Chosen, Re-Rosen Disc Jockey" and again in October 1988, when Sports Radio 66 WFAN premiered.

*Famous line:* "Everybody say Bayyyyyyyybay."

*For more information:* Read *God's Other Son: The Life and Times of Reverend Billy Sol Hargus* by Don Imus.

*In real life:* No one specifically, but a parody of 1950s preachers

### Ross Perot (Larry Kenney)

The "jug-eared little weasel" gives commentary and usually refers to Don as "Larry," referring to Larry King, on whose program he makes many of his announcements, or just "Amus."

*Famous line:* "Larry, let me tell you . . ."

*In real life:* billionaire industrialist, former presidential candidate, and *Larry King Show* guest

### Andy Rooney (Larry Kenney)

Commentator for the *Imus in Washington* network news team. Rooney is frequently called on to give commentary on strange and bizarre things.

*Famous line:* "Look at these news anchors I have lined up on my desk."

*In real life:* commentator for CBS News's *60 Minutes*

### South Lawn (various)
Promotional announcements for the program *South Lawn,* a takeoff on Comedy Central's hit *South Park.* President Clinton plays the character "Fatman" (Cartman), and in every promo someone dies.
*Famous line:* "Oh, my God, they killed . . ."
*In real life:* adult cartoon

### Mike Tyson (Rob Bartlett)
The high-voiced boxer makes an occasional phone call to the Imus show. The jokes range from drinking to ear biting to questioning Imus's manhood.
*Famous line:* "Hello, Missa Trump."
*In real life:* boxer and former felon

### Maya Angelou (Bernard McGuirk)
The famous poet reads poems especially commissioned for the Imus show, sounding a lot like a female Buckwheat.
*In real life:* poet; read poem at first Clinton inauguration.

### Beavis and Bubba (Rob Bartlett and Rob Bartlett)
The childish duo chat about the current goings on. Beavis will harass "Bubba" on any number of stupid things he has done, such as, "At least I didn't marry Hillary."
*Famous line:* "Screw you, Beavis."
*In real life:* MTV cartoon character and president

### Bubba Clinton (Rob Bartlett)
Bubba Clinton sings. In fact, he joined "Hillary" in a duet called "I've Got a Few Babes" to the tune of Sonny and Cher's "I've Got You Babe" and soloed with "I Don't Wanna Lie."

He can also be heard reciting from his diary, recounting made-up stories of interns gone bad, or lashing out at people who have done him wrong, including shots at the I-Man.
*Famous line:* ". . . that jerk Don Imus"
*In real life:* president of the United States

### Blind Mississippi White Boy Pig-Feets Dupree (Rob Bartlett)
Blind is actually far-sighted, but that doesn't sound as good. Blind sings the blues and blows a mean harmonica. He comes

out just in time for the remote broadcasts and brings along a snappy song with him, based around the location, like "The Bangor Blues" or "The Georgia Blues."

*Famous line:* "Got them . . . Blues"

*In real life:* fictional

### Sen. Edward Kennedy (Larry Kenney)

The senator is called on when a Democratic view or the subject of the Kennedys comes up. Whenever he mentions water, a sound effect with car tires screeching, a splash, and a woman crying, "Help, help," is played. This is a not-so-vague reference to the 1969 incident in Chappaquidick when Mary Jo Kopeckne, whom he was driving home, drowned when Kennedy's car crashed off a bridge.

*Famous line:* "Can I get some Chivas over here?"

*In real life:* senior senator from Massachusetts

### Howard Stern (Rob Bartlett)

Will occasionally call in strictly to harass Don, reminding him of his days as a drunk and drug addict while at WNBC.

*Famous line:* "Hey, Don, how's your *Donkey Kong*? Yeah, that was funny."

*In real life:* syndicated radio-show host and CBS radio coworker

### Mark From Milwaukee (Rob Bartlett)

Mark is a psychotically obsessed fan who lives by the Holland Tunnel in New York and wants to meet his idol and to be "just like Don." He will call in to the show and talk so fast that he is barely understandable. We find out that Mark is homicidal and once made the trip all the way to New Mexico just for the chance of working for Fred.

*Famous line:* "HiImusit'sMarkFromMilwaukeei'myour-biggestfan."

*In real life:* fictional, but there may be several borderline fans in the Imus chat or even ones who write books about the radio icon.

### Elvis Presley (Larry Kenney)

The king of rock and roll gives reports and commentary from heaven itself, accompanied by harps and all. Elvis keeps Imus up-to-date on new arrivals and offers various other opinions.

*Famous line:* "How about a cheeseburger, son?"
*In real life:* deceased rock-and-roll singer

## C. Vernon Mason (Al Rosenberg)

African-American lawyer who calls in and comments on news and other events. At one point, this character was having a run-in with Rob Bartlett, saying, "If Rob was having an affair, it would probably be catered," and that he was representing investors of Bartlett's Broadway show. "They want to know if he really needs a new El Dorado to get back and forth to rehearsals."

*Famous line:* "Good moanin', Good moanin', Good moanin' . . ."

*In real life:* New York attorney made famous for his participation in the Tawana Brawley case

## PAST CHARACTERS

## Frank Bruno (Rob Bartlett)

The British boxer plays on his accent and his more "feminine" side, if you will.

*Famous line:* none
*In real life:* former heavyweight contender

## David Brinkley (Don Imus)

Even back in the early seventies, Imus was doing politics with *Imus in Washington,* and "Brinkley" started it all off.

*Famous line:* "This just in to the *Imus in Washington* network newsroom . . ."

*In real life:* famous newsman

## Liz Smith (Rob Bartlett)

Liz was part of the "Double-I Doule U Network Newsroom." (That's *Imus in Washington.*) Contributed some occasional celebrity gossip to the program.

*Famous line:* none
*In real life:* syndicated gossip columnist (and Imus suck-up) in the *New York Post*

## Diane Sawyer (Jane Gennaro)

The female member of the I-I-W network news team

**Spike Lee**
Gives his usual comments as to the mistreatment of African Americans.
*In real life:* lousy movie director and Knicks fan

**Buddy Miyagi (Rob Bartlett)**
One of the first Rob Bartlett characters, Buddy is a Japanese stand-up comic who would tell American jokes in the style of Polish jokes.
*Famous line:* "How many Americans does it take to change a lightbulb? None; they are too fat and lazy."
*Era:* 1986–94

**Hannibal the Cannibal**
A takeoff on the character Hannibal Lecter from *Silence of the Lambs*
*Era:* discontinued after 1991

**Prof. Leonard Jeffries**
Would deliver an Afrocentric view of the world.
*In real life:* New York professor with Afrocentric view of the world

**Crazy Bob (Don Imus)**
Crazy Bob was the Mister Rogers of the Imus program, telling twisted children's stories to the kiddies. Would occasionally tell them to a young girl, one of Don's former girlfriends.
*Famous line:* "Oh, his legs went east, and his tail went west, and that's the part of the story Crazy Bob likes the best."
*Era:* 1973–88

**Judge Hangin' (Don Imus)**
A very early Imus character, he appeared in the early seventies as a soft-drawling 100 percent American for whom police brutality is the "fun part of law enforcement."
*Era:* 1973–77

**Brother Love (Don Imus)**
Another original Imus character, he's a saucy black preacher who advises women in his parish on affairs of the body.

## Geraldo Santana Banana (Larry Chance)

The original political commentator on the *Imus in the Morning* program. Geraldo was described as "vice president and general manager of the *Imus in the Morning* program." Geraldo had a Hispanic accent and was probably based on newsman and Imus friend Geraldo Rivera.

*Famous line:* "Geraldo Santana Banana, thank you bery, bery much."

*Era:* 1970s–88

## Moby Worm (Don Imus)

The reports would come in from throughout the New York tri-state area that Moby Worm—a giant Godzilla-like worm, longer than a city block—was on the loose. He would attack various schools and places like Giants Stadium. At one time he was trapped in one of New York's tunnels after thinking he could be amorous with it. Coverage usually anchored by Capt. Frank Reed (a former WNBC deejay), who would die in every episode.

*Famous line:* chomping sounds and occasionally synthe-sized words

*Era:* 1979–80s

## Earl C. Watkins (Al Rosenberg)

The predecessor of "Mark from Milwaukee" was "Earl C. Watkins," a businessman from Naugatuck, Connecticut. Earl would tell stories about his latest business ventures, all made from natural nauga. (They looked like little ottomans.)

*Famous line:* Imus: "Earl C. Watkins, he's our man." Earl: "Number-one *Imus in the Morning* fan."

*Era:* 1980s–85

## Rex the Wonder Dog

While he never actually appeared on the *Imus in the Morning* program, lots of New Yorkers remembered hearing the announcements of the coming of Rex. It's doubtful Rex ever would have made it, mostly because the story of the dog had its roots in a dirty joke that, if you must read it, is recounted in the chapter "Imus Branches Out."

*Famous line:* "Rex the Wonder Dog, coming soon to *Imus in the Morning*"

**Stella Steel (Roz Frank)**
Stella was a sleazy gossip reporter, talking about the trash that happened to New York's rich and famous.

*Famous line:* "A hot meal, a cheap deal. Thank you, Stella Steel."

## Gone but Not Totally Forgotten Older Characters

Sal Monella
Dr. Schultz
Skip and Muffy
Shecky Bhuta

## Other People Parodied on the Show

Barbara Walters, hostess of ABC News's *20/20*
Barbara Bush, first lady
Audrey Hepburn, actress
Frank Sinatra, chairman of the board
Clarence Thomas, Supreme Court justice
George Bush, president of the United States
Jay Leno, host of *The Tonight Show*
Madonna, singer; sang "Exploitable Girl" in 1991 on show
Joe Pepitone, New York Yankee player
Jeane Kirkpatrick, U.S. ambassador to the United States
Pee Wee Herman, Paul Reuben's character; kids-show star
Joey Buttafucco, auto-body-shop owner and famous adulterer
John Gotti, the don of dons
Richard Petty, race-car driver
Mr. T, television actor
Manuel Noriega, dictator
Leona Helmsley, hotel owner

# 23
# IMUS TIME LINE

**H**ere's a list of important events throughout Imus's life:

*1904*   John Donald Imus Sr. (father) born

*1910*   Frances E. Moore Imus (mother) born

*July 23, 1940*   John Donald Imus Jr. born in Riverside, California

*1942*   Frederic Imus (brother) born

*1940–57*   cattle ranches with family and brother Fred in Prescott, Arizona, on a 35,000-acre ranch called the Willows.

*1955*   John Senior and Mary Imus divorce.

*1953–57*   attends Scottsdale, Arizona, High School; drops out.

*1957–59*   joins U.S. Marine Corps, is stationed at Camp Pendleton, and becomes a bugler in the marine band.

*1959–61*   tries, along with Fred, to break into recording industry; ends up homeless. Fred and Don perform songs under the stage names Jay Jay Imus and Freddie Ford.

*1961*   works in Arizona Uranium and Copper Mines.

*1962*   John Donald Imus Sr. dies.

*Early 1960s*   Imus marries first wife, Harriet.

*1964*   Deirdre Coleman is born.

*1964–66*   brakeman for Southern Pacific Railroad; leaves with back injury after train wreck and engine turnover.

*1966–68*  attends Don Martin School of Broadcasting in Los Angeles; does not graduate because he still owed the school five hundred dollars.

*June 1, 1968*  premiers on radio on Palmdale, California, station KUTY: salary, eighty dollars per week; runs for Congress versus Barry Goldwater Jr.

*1969*  KJOY—Stockton, California; salary $800 per month; conducts an Eldridge Cleaver look-alike contest and is fired after ten months.

*1969*  KXOA—Sacramento, California; does 1,200 Hamburgers bit, which leads to FCC's regulations for disclosure of phone calls on air; begins to include characters on his show, including the Right Reverend Dr. Billy Sol Hargus; receives *Billboard* Medium Market Personality of the Year Award.

*1970*  WGAR—Cleveland; named *Billboard* Major Market Disk Jockey of the Year.

*December 1971*  premieres on 66 WNBC-AM in New York; starting salary estimated at $80,000 per year; age: thirty-one.

*1972*  Charles McCord joins *Imus in the Morning* team as occasional newsman and writer.

*Early 1970s*  begins to photograph Southwest with brother.

*1973*  Larry Kenney joins *Imus in the Morning*. Larry portrays characters such as Richard Nixon, Elvis Presley, and Walter Cronkite.

*1973*  misses one hundred days of work.

*August 1977*  is fired from WNBC.

*September 3, 1979*  returns from Cleveland to WNBC; starts with Billy Sol Hargus bit; Lyndon Abel, producer.

*1979*  leaves wife and four daughters in Cleveland; divorce soon follows.

*1980*  votes for Reagan for president.

*1981*  *God's Other Son* original release.

*February 1981*   mother, Frances, dies.

*September 1982*   Howard Stern joins the lineup at WNBC.

*1983*   dumps coke and joins AA.

*1983*   Bernard McGuirk starts as *Imus in the Morning* producer.

*1984*   again votes for Reagan for president.

*January 1, 1985*   premieres as the first "veejay" on brand-new cable channel "Video Hits-One," or VH-1.

*September 1985*   Howard Stern leaves WNBC.

*1986*   Rob Bartlett joins Imus show as frequent guest; becomes permanent contract player with WFAN move in 1988.

*1987*   *God's Other Son* paperback-book tour; goes on nine-day binge; checks into Hazelden in West Palm Beach.

*October 7, 1988*   stays at 660 AM when WFAN moves to WNBC's old frequency; switches broadcast on WNBC-TV New York from Shea Stadium parking lot prior to Mets-Dodgers play-off game; starts 66 WFAN broadcast with Billy Sol Hargus bit.

*1988*   votes for George Bush for president.

*1990*   TCF radiothon starts.

*January 1991*   buys Southport home for $1.275 million.

*August 1991*   trips over first base in Special Olympics benefit softball game.

*November 1991*   *Connecticut* magazine publishes article; estimates Imus's salary now at $1.5 million per year.

*1991*   Gulf War provides some of Imus's biggest ratings when he works more politics into show; *God's Other Son* is rereleased.

*June 17, 1992*   Imus serves as governor of Connecticut for a day.

*Spring 1992*   Gov. Bill Clinton appears on Imus program during New York primary, covered by *Nightline.*

*1992*   votes for Bill Clinton for president.

*May 1993* gets lost basketball Indiana Pacers' playbook and broadcasts plays on the air.

*July 1993* begins syndication in Tampa, Boston, and Washington, D.C.

*August 1993* Imus's lung collapses, and he is twice hospitalized.

*February 17, 1994* President Clinton appears on Imus show for possibly the last time.

*March 1994* Imus becomes engaged to marry Deirdre Coleman (twenty-nine).

*December 17, 1994* marries Deirdre Coleman.

*1994* *God's Other Son* on audiotape is released.

*April 4, 1995* Sen. Al D'Amato (R-NY) insults Judge Lance Ito during Imus program.

*April 6, 1995* Sen. Al D'Amato apologizes to Ito and Japanese Americans on the Senate floor.

*January 4, 1996* *God's Other Son* audiotape nominated for Grammy for Best Spoken Comedy Album.

*March 21, 1996* "The Speech From Hell"; Imus gives a speech to the Washington Radio-Television Correspondents Association's dinner.

*April 1996* inducted into National Association of Broadcasters Hall of Fame.

*May 1996* Minneapolis bus driver causes controversy when he forces eight-year-old to listen to Imus.

*September 1996* *Imus on MSNBC* premieres. MSNBC simulcasts three hours of the radio show on a daily basis.

*September 1996* Wisconsin TV station refuses Imus ad.

*October 18, 1996* broadcasts from Milwaukee.

*December 9, 1996* *Broadcasting and Cable* announces that Imus has signed a new seven-year deal with Infinity Broadcasting; salary estimated at $3 million per year.

*1996*   votes for Bob Dole for president.

*April 1997*   *Time* magazine names Imus one of the 25 Most Influential Americans, along with comic-strip character Dilbert and talk-show host Rosie O'Donnell.

*May–June 1997*   *Two Guys, Four Corners,* a book of Southwest photography by Don Imus and Fred Imus, is published by Villard.

*March 1998*   establishes the Imus Ranch Foundation and begins to develop a ranch in New Mexico for Tomorrow's Children's Fund kids.

*July 3, 1998*   Fredric Wyatt Imus is born, son of Don Imus and Deirdre Coleman-Imus.

# AFTERWORD

This concludes the informational and painstakingly tedious portion of the *Everything Imus* book. The remainder of the book will probably contain an index and perhaps even a few blank pages that you can rip out and use to write a list of books you probably should have read instead of *Everything Imus.* Perhaps they can be used to write hate mail to all those involved in perpetrating this hideous creation and launching it on an unsuspecting general public.

If you skipped ahead to see if this was some kind of murder mystery and Imus died in the end, I'm sorry; he is alive and well. If you have actually read this far, perhaps those extra pages can be ripped from the book and folded to make lovely paper swans or other items during arts and crafts class at the happy home. In more severe cases, you should consider a long vacation away from reality. If you are waiting for something funny, you are still waiting.

If you really want something funny, look for the *Imus in the Morning* program, heard on over 100 radio stations and MSNBC every weekday morning. Check your local listings for when it's on. Remember, there is only one Imus, and I ain't him. Thank God.

## INTERNET RESOURCES MENTIONED IN AND RELATED TO *EVERYTHING IMUS* (ACCURATE AS OF AUGUST 31, 1998)

All can be found at http://everythingimus.com

Jim Reed, author    E-mail: jimreed@everythingimus.com

The Super Imus Links page    http://imonthe.net/imus

The Auto Body Express    http://autobodyexpress.com

Jack's *Imus in the Morning* page    http://kajor.com/imus

*Imus in the Morning* on MSNBC    http://imus.msnbc.com

Imus Usenet News Group    alt.fan.don-imus

Rob Bartlett Usenet News Group    alt.fan.rob-bartlett

Rob Bartlett's Home Page    http://robshow.com

Imus-Fans' Mailing List    E-Mail:imus-list@kajor.com

Tips on Trips Travel    http://www.trip007.com

Ramsey Nursery    http://growbaby.com

# INDEX